THE MANAGER'S POCKET GUIDE TO

Knowledge Management

by Kathleen Foley Curley
and
Barbara Kivowitz

HRD PRESS
Amherst, Massachusetts

Published by:
HRD Press
22 Amherst Road
1-800-822-2801
(U.S. and Canada)
1-413-253-3488
1-413-253-3490 (Fax)
www.hrdpress.com

ISBN 0-87425-641-0

Cover design by Eileen Klockars
Production services by Anctil Virtual Office
Editorial services by Sally M. Farnham

Acknowledgements

We would like to thank our colleagues at Lotus Institute and at Lotus. The pioneering research we did together on the many aspects of knowledge management and organizational learning greatly informed our thinking.

TABLE OF CONTENTS

Knowledge is now a core business asset. What forces and drivers are making knowledge management essential to business strategy?

A business definition of knowledge clarifies the relationship among data, information, and knowledge and provides a foundation for effective knowledge management.

To make knowledge usable, and realize its value, businesses develop processes for creating it, distributing it, and applying it.

What is knowledge management? How does it link to organizational learning? Using the RICE model, a framework of Responsiveness, Innovation, Competency, and Efficiency, organizations can link knowledge management and organizational learning and focus their knowledge management strategy on building core competencies.

Chapter Five

Nine specific action areas rooted in the RICE model provide
targeted ways to assess and build competency, use knowledge
to make processes more efficient, increase responsiveness, and
nurture innovation.

Chapter Six

A practical plan and roadmap lay out the steps for knowledge management implementation. A scenario describes
how one (fictitious) company puts it all together to develop
a knowledge management strategy for managing their
knowledge assets to expand their core competency and
win significant competitive advantage.

Introduction

I0 Myths about Knowledge Management

As knowledge management becomes more widely adopted, misconceptions about what it is and isn't have also become more widespread. Here are the top 10 myths about knowledge management:

1. *Knowledge management is an end unto itself.* In fact, while creating new knowledge, organizing it so others can use it, and passing it on to succeeding generations is a defining human trait, business organizations should use knowledge management to build market value and competitive strength.

2. *Knowledge management is just for professional services firms and other "intellectual" businesses.* Not so. As we will see in Chapter 1, knowledge is a big percentage of the value of all goods and services produced in every industry.

3. *Knowledge management just means hiring smart people.* While it is true that people are the main sources of knowledge, it is what people do, not just what they know, that adds value to firms.

4. *Knowledge management means implementing expensive technology.* Technology certainly plays a key role—especially in distributing knowledge. But technology alone will not improve a company's knowledge management or make it more competitive.

5. *Knowledge management means creating huge, unwieldy databases.* It's true that many firms follow the "Grandma's attic" approach to saving any information that might possibly be useful someday. But these are not the firms that get

I

business value from their knowledge. Knowledge yields value when your people know where it is, know how to get at it, know it will help them, and join in keeping it current, practical, and useful.

6. *Knowledge management is a "Field of Dreams"—just build it, and they will come.* In that movie, a mystical voice tells the main character that if he builds a baseball field in his backyard, the legends of baseball will appear. That voice won't help you with knowledge management. Building a new technology or process for creating and applying knowledge is not enough to inspire participation in knowledge management or yield business results.

7. *Good knowledge management is driven by a good Chief Knowledge Officer (CKO) or Chief Learning Officer (CLO).* The creation, distribution, and application of knowledge drives the value of an organization's goods and services and determines its market value. Whether you recognize and cultivate them or not, your knowledge processes are at the heart of your business. They can't be left in the hands of one executive, however effective.

8. *Knowledge management is just for Americans.* Because the marketplace is global, the creation, distribution, and application of knowledge must also be global—not confined to one region, language, or culture.

9. *Knowledge management is not like other good management practices and processes.* Managing knowledge does not mean reinventing management. The elements of effective financial management, such as building theoretical knowledge, developing a shared vocabulary, and implementing best practice and processes, also drive effective knowledge management.

10. *Knowledge management is a fad.* The term "knowledge management" might fade away or be replaced. But the enormous contribution of knowledge to business value will only grow and the activities that create value from knowledge will always be vital to success.

If you have had suspicions about knowledge management, you have a lot of company. Until recently, you were certainly in the vast majority. Perhaps, by choosing to read this book, you are moving from suspicion to curiosity. So are many managers and companies. They are coming to realize that there is substance behind the hype. Knowledge—about customers, about the market, about core processes, about how things get done, about who knows what—is a core business asset that, when well managed, returns significant value.

Early on, knowledge management was viewed as visionary by a small number of innovators and as unimportant, frivolous, or even spurious by the majority of researchers and business people. Professional services firms were part of the first wave to take knowledge management seriously and give it a solid foothold. The business of these firms is the creation and transfer of knowledge. They realized that they needed better methods and technology for managing their knowledge —the core asset upon which their credibility, competitiveness, and longevity rest. They were soon followed by a cadre of early adopters, including larger companies in financial services, communications, and manufacturing, as well as large government agencies.

Now knowledge management is becoming mainstream in many industries and is spreading from large firms to medium-sized ones. In fact, at a recent World Economic Forum, 97 percent of chief executives surveyed stated that knowledge management is critical to the success of their companies. IDC (an industry research group) estimates that "worldwide spending for knowledge management services—including consulting,

3

implementation, support, outsourcing, and training—will grow from $776 million in 1998 to over $8 billion by 2003."[1] Other estimates are even higher.

As knowledge management spreads through industry, its definition is expanding beyond aspects such as data mining, advanced search technology, and business intelligence. Concepts such as explicit and tacit knowledge, social networks, communities of practice, and virtual teams, have emerged as legitimate components of a knowledge management architecture. Learnings from the trenches have taught us that a hospitable cultural environment in which people share ideas and communicate freely is as important as a robust technical infrastructure.

In this book, we define knowledge management as much more than a set of tools or processes or the implementation of powerful technology. Knowledge management is **the conscious management of a key corporate asset—knowledge—for the purpose of advancing organizational learning, strengthening the organization's ability to sustain and expand its core competencies, and securing competitive advantage.** We realize this definition is an earful. As you read this book, we will unravel it for you and help you find ways to get started on knowledge management.

This book is intended to be both informative and practical. We emphasize strategy and practice and classes of solutions, rather than focusing on specific technologies (which change too fast). We offer some key frameworks, or lenses, through which you can understand, and apply, the main concepts inherent in a knowledge management strategy. We will emphasize three critical principles:

- Knowledge management is about the conscious management of the business asset, knowledge.

- The management of this asset is about the management of both *information* and *relationships.*

4

- The ultimate goal of knowledge management is the systematic advancement of *organizational learning* so that the core competencies (the true competitive advantage) grow stronger and more widespread throughout the organization.

We will explain these concepts in more detail in the book's early chapters. In later chapters, we will offer you practical guidance for applying these concepts and for getting started with knowledge management in your own organization.

What we hope to do in this book is offer you a sense of lessons learned to date and some practical ground rules for getting started. As the story goes, someone once stopped a New Yorker on a street corner and asked her how to get to Carnegie Hall. Her answer? "Practice." Our advice to you as you read this book is to take these learnings—and practice them! Apply them in your own environments; learn as you go; keep what works and let go of what doesn't.

Kathleen Foley Curley
Barbara Kivowitz

Endnotes

[1] Greg Dyer, "KM Crosses the Chasm," *Knowledge Management* magazine (US), March 2000, 50.

Chapter I
Knowledge Management: Why Now?

"The effective management of knowledge is the key management challenge of the late twentieth and early twenty-first century," observes Peter Drucker. Why is this so? After all, knowledge has always been important for business success. Medieval merchants and sea captains closely guarded navigational lore. Inventions and patents were vital to the growth of the American industrial economy in the nineteenth century. The promise of better information management has been driving the computer industry since the 1950s.

As vital as knowledge has been all along, powerful forces are converging in our time to move it ahead of land, capital, raw materials, and technology as the key to competitive advantage. These forces drive—and are driven by—an ever-faster pace of change. In previous eras, a trade secret, an invention, or other piece of highly valuable business knowledge could yield a competitive edge that endured for many years. Today, that "knowledge edge" has a much shorter life span.

Consider, for example, typewriters and computers as writing tools. A well-made typewriter of 1940 was just as useful in 1950—or 1960 (barring wear and tear). To stay ahead in the typewriter business, typewriter firms made incremental improvements from year to year while adapting to one major change, the emergence of electric typewriters. Remington, Smith-Corona, and Royal were all big American brands throughout those years. When it comes to computers, only a technological nostalgist would use a computer and word-processing software from 1990 in 2000. And many companies that competed in the personal computer and word-processing software markets of 1990 are memories today and will be utterly forgotten by 2010.

In this chapter, we explore six of the forces that have come together to change the way knowledge contributes to business success and sharply compress the time frame within which new knowledge has business value. These forces have forged a business environment in which creating new knowledge and managing its rapid application are the keys to competitive advantage, profitability, and market capitalization.

1. Information is being created and shared at an unprecedented rate.

Knowledge is doubling about every seven years. In technical fields, half of what students learn in their first year of college is obsolete by the time they graduate.[1]

The knowledge explosion has two facets: where it is coming from, and how people access it. On the source side, for reasons too complex to explore here, we are benefiting from a fifty-year-long boom in scientific and industrial research that has been accelerated even further in the past fifteen years by ever-faster, ever-cheaper computing power. The Human Genome Project is just one example of a major research undertaking that has gone much farther, much faster, than anyone thought possible even ten years ago. On the access side, awareness of the value of managing knowledge coincides with the huge growth in the installed base of personal computers, networking, and the widespread distribution of digital media.[2]

Currently, there are at least a billion pages on the Internet. In 1997, there were approximately 300 million. The total number of Web users around the globe, estimated at 320 million in 2000, is expected to reach 720 million by 2005.

2. Making sense of information is the challenge now.

Economists long held that getting information was a key constraint in creating efficient markets. It's no longer so. With the rapid rise of information technology and the flowering of the Internet and the Web, the bottleneck now is extracting useful content and making sense of it. In financial services, for example, a staggering amount of potentially useful information is instantly accessible to any trader or portfolio manager. Trading operations must find ways to manage and prioritize information flow to remain competitive. An hour's lead time integrating information and making a move on the trading floor is a huge competitive advantage.

Whether your time frame is an hour, a week, a month, or a year, making sense out of information and converting that sense-making into action is the process of creating, distributing, and applying knowledge. In this book, we will provide you with a framework for managing knowledge that helps you focus on approaches that can really help your organization.

3. Knowledge is the key value added to goods and services.

Knowledge, or the know-how to turn information into action, is becoming an increasing percentage of the value of all goods and services produced. In the United States, service industries accounted for 77 percent of employment and 75 percent of all GNP in the early 1990s. Service activities—including advertising, marketing, and logistics—contribute most of the value added in manufacturing and constitute between 65 and 75 percent of most manufacturers' costs.[3]

Traditionally, companies treated these kinds of costs as overhead and tried to keep them to a minimum. Today, firms increasingly recognize the opportunity to be more competitive through an investment in service-based labor. Investing in marketing and advertising can differentiate the product in the eye of the beholder. The new computers Apple has introduced since 1998 aren't all that different on the inside from previous Apple products. But they look different on the outside. And through Apple's "Think Different" marketing campaign, they are strongly linked to the idea of being different. In manufacturing companies, supply-chain management—which is all about managing the flow of information and knowledge across organizational boundaries—has been instrumental in reducing costs, inventories, and cycle times for commodity businesses that benefit from every fractional improvement in efficiency.

Focusing on the customer is another knowledge-intensive activity that can yield an excellent return on investment. Back in the 1950s, IBM Chairman Thomas Watson, Jr., was a firm believer in "systems knowledge"—customer service and technical support—and attention to these functions helped IBM attain preeminence in the days of the mainframe computer.[4] Sir Colin Marshall, formerly the chairman of British Airways, noted that the "commodity mind-set is to think that a business is merely performing a function—in our case, transporting people from point A to point B on time and at the lowest possible price." To go beyond that, according to Sir Colin, is to "compete on the basis of providing an experience that attempts to transform air travel into a respite from the traveler's normally frenetic life."[5] Under his leadership, British Airways studied what its customers wanted, integrated its learnings into its flight experience, shook off its reputation for poor service, and become a preferred airline for international travelers.

The Web is being used as a tool for gaining increased customer knowledge that can be converted into personalized experience. American Airlines upgraded its website in June 1998, enabling customers to enter personalized options for air travel, and offering attractive discounts on numerous flights. After this initiative, American Airlines had one of the most heavily trafficked airline reservation sites on the Web with $6 million worth of bookings per week and increased revenues for American Airlines Advantage partners.[6] At the website of Land's End, a form of instant messaging enables a live Land's End employee to "step in" and offer assistance to online shoppers whose clicking patterns suggest that they are having trouble finding what they need.

All of these areas offer real opportunities to win competitive advantage by creating and applying knowledge. But they require structured, focused approaches to knowledge management to filter out inessentials and zero in on what will work for your products, processes, services, customers, and brand. Land's End's personalized Web shopping help is a targeted, logical, and smart way to extend the firm's excellent reputation for customer service.

4. **The market values knowledge more than physical assets.**

Investors are highly attuned to the shift away from physical assets to knowledge and the innovative capability it supports. One way to think of the business value of knowledge is in terms of a formula known as Tobin's Q. Named after James Tobin, a Nobel-prize-winning economist, Tobin's Q is the ratio of a company's value in the securities markets to the value of its tangible assets. If the company's market value exceeds its asset value, investors are presumably valuing an intangible asset such as knowledge. (Tobin suggests other possibilities as well, such as good will or a monopoly position.)[7]

11

> *"All the value of this company is in its people. If you burned down all our plants and we just kept our people and our information files, we would soon be as strong as ever. Take away our people, and we might never recover."*
>
> Thomas Watson, Jr., Chairman, IBM, 1952–1971

Consider, for example, how investors value GM and Microsoft. GM's market value in November 2000 was approximately $30 billion. Its assets in 1999 were valued at $405 billion. Microsoft's market value in November 2000 was approximately $361 billion, against assets of $37 billion. In other words, while GM's market value was one-thirteenth of its assets, Microsoft's market value was ten times its assets. GM is saddled with tangible assets, including an enormous physical plant and a worldwide inventory of cars, whose replacement cost is far greater than the company's value to investors. Microsoft, on the other hand, is rich in intangible value, generated by its software and the marketing know-how of its staff—and, no doubt, by its near-monopoly in some of its markets.

Tobin's Q can also be read as a measure of how well the market perceives the current management team's ability to exploit these assets. Here again, companies in knowledge-intensive industries are favored in the market. SBC Communications, a successful Baby Bell with significant infrastructure, has assets of $83 billion and a market value (in November 2000) of $194 billion—a ratio of more than two to one, reflecting investors' sense that SBC has the know-how to succeed in the rapidly evolving telecommunications industry. Alcoa, a well-managed company in a process-intensive, commodity industry, has assets of $17 billion and a market value of $24 billion. The lower ratio reflects, in part, the limited enthusiasm investors feel about the value of a traditional industrial firm, however well-run.

5. Globalization requires new knowledge-coordinating structures.

The globalization of business is a phenomenon that is easier to cite than describe. Many companies are globalizing in one way or another, but the process is different for each. Globalization, for example, means entering new markets. European media conglomerates are buying American media assets and competing in American markets, and vice versa. GM is gearing up to sell an economy car in China (based on an economy sedan from Opel, a German line of the Michigan-based company). Financial services firms, from Fidelity to Scudder & Zurich Kemper, are marketing investment instruments (modified to meet specific regulations) across national borders.

Globalization means pursuing new resources—raw materials, labor, manufacturing capabilities, and knowledge—anywhere in the world you can. Chevron is painstakingly securing access to Russian oil and gas reserves. Clothing companies from the Gap to Old Navy and J.Crew to L.L. Bean farm out the making of their khakis, t-shirts, and the like to a plethora of developing nations. U.S. software companies get programming help in a tight job market from programmers in India, a country with a strong mathematical heritage. Business-to-Business (B2B) websites with auction/bidding capabilities enable truly global market exchange while breaking down traditional organizational structures.

Globalization means new kinds of alliances, partnerships, and joint ventures that also give companies access to markets and resources. These shared enterprises require collaboration and knowledge exchange between companies that may have been competitors in the past.

These examples only scratch the surface of the drive to globalize that is changing many companies. Without new kinds of knowledge-coordinating structures, none of these new globalized processes—in production, marketing, sales, human resources, and many other realms—will work very well. Teams must be able to form and share knowledge and results without gathering in one place or even having a physical home base. Departments, divisions, and regional structures need to shed old habits of information-hoarding and collaborate to develop best practices that can then be customized by function or region. Companies need to learn how to share knowledge and resources in alliances and joint ventures that bring people from different organizational and social cultures together. Companies are also grappling with how to make the most of the Web, which replaces hierarchical information exchange with a dynamic, horizontal flow and enables fluid, team-based collaboration.

6. **New organizational and decision-making structures depend on knowledge management.**

Many companies have changed enormously in the past fifteen years. Waves of downsizing, reengineering, quality management, and delayering, not to mention mergers, demergers, consolidations, and spin-offs, have seriously weakened the command-and-control environment of the old industrial giants.

In disrepair, too, are the cumbersome, hierarchical planning, analysis, and decision-making structures that used to support corporate strategy. Now companies know that they need to be nimble, adaptive, responsive, and customer-focused.

They need to be prepared to master new competencies and markets, and do so in a team-based, project-focused way that gets results without excessive corporate guidance. Rather than using single-point forecasts and strategic goals, they need to stay on top of multiple objectives and shifting priorities. Yet they are still evolving the support structures that can provide consistency and efficiency for these new ways of working.

Knowledge management is the keystone of those structures—and companies are showing an awareness of that fact in their budgets. On the technology side of knowledge management alone, companies are expected to be spending $35 billion a year to implement systems by 2004. The e-mail and intranet systems now in place already seem awkward and inefficient to many users who must prioritize, read, sort, respond to, and attempt to file dozens, if not hundreds of e-mails every day on topics from the sublime to the ridiculous and laboriously click through stale intranet pages in search of useful information. Often, the easiest thing to do is still to pick up the phone and call the unofficial expert everyone in your group calls—even though "on-call expert" isn't in her job description. That's the irony of the current environment: the more rapidly technology changes, the more individual talent and capability matter.

Take a Moment

Have the changes sweeping through industry reached your organization? The following questions can help you determine the extent to which knowledge management is becoming or could become a key to competitive advantage in your organization. Total up the numbers of your answers. The higher your total score, the more important knowledge management could be in your business environment.

- What percentage of your organization's workers are involved in knowledge work or knowledge services?

  (1) 25 percent or less
  (2) 50 percent
  (3) 75 percent
  (4) 90 percent
  (5) More than 90 percent

- What percentage of the wholesale price of your product is in the cost of raw materials?

  (1) 75 percent or more
  (2) 50 percent
  (3) 25 percent
  (4) 10 percent
  (5) Less than 10 percent

- To be an expert in your domain, how rapidly do you have to update your skills?

  (1) Every five years
  (2) Every three years
  (3) Every two years
  (4) Every year
  (5) More than once a year

- Look at the industry leader in your competitive environment. What percent of the market capitalization comes from tangible assets or book value?

  (1) 100 percent
  (2) 75 percent
  (3) 50 percent
  (4) 25 percent
  (5) 10 percent or less

- What percentage of your current product offering is less than five years old?

    (1) 10 percent
    (2) 25 percent
    (3) 50 percent
    (4) 75 percent
    (5) 90 percent

- What percentage of the human talent required to create your product is outsourced or obtained through alliances with other companies?

    (1) 10 percent
    (2) 25 percent
    (3) 50 percent
    (4) 75 percent
    (5) 90 percent

- What percentage of your firm's revenues comes from markets outside your home country?

    (1) 10 percent
    (2) 25 percent
    (3) 50 percent
    (4) 75 percent
    (5) 90 percent or more

Taking the Next Step

If knowledge management is so important, where does a company begin? Assessing the importance of knowledge to your enterprise is a start. Equally important is defining the knowledge challenge and the steps you need to take in terms that make sense for your business. In the following chapters, we will take you through a business definition of knowledge and knowledge management and construct a practical framework for aligning knowledge management efforts with company objectives. While we talk a lot about definitions and structures, our focus is really people. In the end, knowledge management is about giving people the tools they need to do their best for your company, helping them share their best thinking, and bringing them together in effective, productive teams and communities that bring success—and, we hope, enjoyment and passion—to the pursuit of business goals.

Recap

In this chapter we have described how several powerful forces have come together to create a new business environment. In this environment, creating knowledge and managing its rapid application have become the critical success factors for achieving competitive advantage, profitability, and market capitalization. The forces creating this new environment are:

- The explosion of new knowledge

- The urgent need to quickly understand and apply new knowledge

- The rise of knowledge as the key value added to goods and services

- Financial markets that value knowledge over physical assets

- The globalization of markets

- The appearance of new team-based organizational structures

Building effective collaboration and knowledge coordinating mechanisms has become key to taking advantage of the global marketplace.

Endnotes

[1] Davis, Stan, and J. Botkin, "The Coming of Knowledge Based Business," *Harvard Business Review,* Sept-Oct. 1994, 170. Reprint #94505.

[2] CAP Ventures report.

[3] James Brian Quinn, *The Intelligent Enterprise: A Knowledge and Service Based Paradigm for Industry.*

[4] Brown University website, November 2000.

[5] "An Interview with Sir Colin Marshall," *Harvard Business Review,* November-December 1995.

[6] "Leveraging Knowledge" GIGA Conference, March 16–18, 1999, Walt Disney World, Florida.

[7] Interview with James Tobin, *The Region,* Federal Reserve Bank of Minneapolis, December 1996.

Chapter 2
What Is Knowledge?

Up until now, we have been using the word "knowledge" as a generic, dictionary term, a word everyone knows and understands. We have been using knowledge in its colloquial sense—either something useful that an individual knows, or something useful that many people know in common about a particular subject and that has been collected and validated. An individual artist possesses knowledge about the use of her particular medium. The art world shares knowledge about a historic artistic style such as Impressionism or Cubism.

> *Webster's* New Collegiate Dictionary *defines knowledge as: "cognizance. The fact or condition of knowing something with familiarity gained through experience or association. Acquaintance with or understanding of a science, art, or technique."*

In business, where knowledge is a core economic asset, its meaning takes on new aspects. As an economic resource, business knowledge has value in and of itself and can add value to other existing resources. It can be acquired, developed, measured, and lost, like other tangible corporate assets. For businesses to use knowledge as they use other assets, they need to have a systematic way to define and analyze it. In this chapter, we will provide you with a definition of knowledge that fits business situations and a way to analyze its components for business use.

To help managers understand how to access the value of their company's knowledge resources, this chapter will define knowledge in a business context and outline its dimensions. We will give knowledge a form and structure that is appropriate for the business world.

Acquiring Knowledge Assets

When Ford Motor Company bought the automotive division of Volvo, Ford acquired more than assembly plants, office buildings, inventory, and other tangible assets. A highly respected tradition of automotive know-how, embodied in the design, work processes, and employee skills that help make Volvo cars, became an asset for Ford. Ford could choose to cultivate and preserve this tradition within the Volvo division, develop ways to transfer Volvo knowledge to other Ford divisions, or make other business issues the priority and thereby diminish or even lose Volvo's knowledge assets.

Form: What Knowledge Looks Like

Jacob Needleman, a contemporary philosopher, has developed a model of knowledge that is very useful for managing knowledge in a business context. In Needleman's model, degrees of understanding—which we can represent as layers—constitute a pyramid of knowledge. These layers of knowledge are:

- data
- information
- knowledge
- wisdom

While these levels can be viewed and managed independently, they are more often intertwined and cumulative. Volvo, for example, possesses an enormous trove of data on how collisions affect cars and the people in them. This data can be organized in terms of information about collisions and distilled into highly valuable knowledge about building safer, more damage-resistant cars.

Understanding the differences among data, information, and knowledge—and how they connect—is very important for the business management of knowledge assets. In the following pages, we look more closely at each layer of the knowledge pyramid. (For the purposes of a business discussion about the value of knowledge, we will not maintain wisdom as a separate level, but incorporate it into the knowledge layer.)

The Knowledge Pyramid

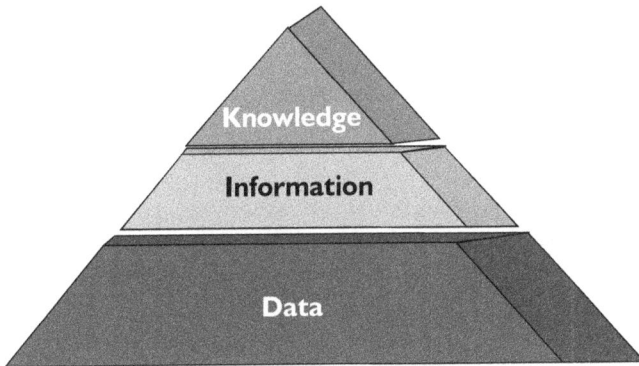

Data

Data is the foundation of knowledge. If we imagine knowledge creation as a process (like making a cake, a car, or a book), data is the raw material extracted from the business environment— ingredients, elements, components, facts. Data can be thought of as the observable facts of a situation or the separate ingredients that make up an event. Take a sales slip, for example. The time stamp, the date, the location, the cash register, the cashier, the amount, the method of payment, the things purchased, the price of each, the total price, the store location, the tax—all are bits of data that the cash register is designed to capture every time a purchase occurs. Or suppose you are travelling by plane. On some airlines, monitors show passengers the air speed, the temperature outside, the distance traveled, and the time left until the plane lands. These are bits of data—facts about the situation. In cooking, data is the ingredients—the number of cups of flour or teaspoons of salt. In music, data could be the notes in a score—separate, intact elements that contribute to a musical composition. Each note, in and of itself, is not the music. But there would be no music without each note.

In a business setting, data can be revenue numbers, measures of cost or savings, employee turnover figures, or a vast multitude of other factual tidbits. Data enables companies to measure and assess their value and demonstrate net worth. Data is neutral. A single piece of data, or a mass of unstructured data, in and of itself, doesn't convey any particular meaning. It is, however, the essential building block for the rest of the pyramid and provides the basis for the next level of knowledge—information. Data becomes useful when it is placed in some kind of context that turns it into information.

From a business perspective, managers need to ensure that the right data is being collected and forwarded to the right places. Data needs to be noted, checked for accuracy, tracked, and updated. A bank, for example, must be able to document and trace every change that occurs in the status of its assets and its customers' assets. If you are an automobile manufacturer, you need to make sure that the number of parts in the warehouse matches the number of parts ordered. A hospital needs to document whether a nurse has given a patient 100 mg. of a medication, or 1,000 mg.

Information

Information adds value to data. It surrounds the data with keys or clues to the data's significance, thereby making it usable. In fact, usability is one of the key distinctions between data and information. Information is data placed in a specific context or structured to yield order and meaning.

In music, the raw data of notes becomes meaningful information on a staff marked with a key, a tempo, and other elements of a musical score. The staff and the sequencing of the notes make the notes usable. The raw material of data has been converted into something an individual can make sense of and use to take action—in this case, think through or play a piece of music. In a business context, the conversion of data to information helps people make decisions, solve problems, or come up with valuable new ideas.

Think back to that sales slip. Each piece of data—the date, the sales tax, items purchased, the location—needs other data and some sort of larger context to acquire meaning and value. Suppose the slip was for a birthday present for your spouse. To you, the total amount spent is what matters—because you used a debit card and need to record the transaction in your checkbook or compare it with your next statement. To your spouse, the date and time are of great interest, since the purchase appears to have taken place 38 minutes before the birthday party began. To the company that manufactured the gift, several contexts could be valuable:

- Location (How is this product selling in this zip code?)

- Time of year (What sort of seasonal sales patterns are typical with this product?)

- Price (What is the markup from wholesale and how does that relate to pricing strategies?)

- Personal buying patterns (How does this purchase on this credit card compare with other purchases on it? What interests, spending levels, or other consumer habits are revealed?)

Information Is Power

In the 1940s, atomic research was underway in the United States on the Manhattan Project. The main focus of this research, led by scientists such as Neils Bohr, Enrico Fermi, Richard Feynman, and Robert Oppenheimer, was the creation of an atomic bomb.

The project was purposely split among several locations, including Chicago, Illinois; Los Alamos, New Mexico; and Oak Ridge, Tennessee. At each site, the scientists and their research were further divided and segregated. In essence, the data produced by researchers was purposely compartmentalized so that it would remain merely data. Most of the researchers could not aggregate and organize the data. They could not turn it into usable information or knowledge. And, therefore, they could not compromise the security of the project, either on purpose or by accident. Only a handful of people on the leadership team could access all the information and understand what it meant.

Businesses are often awash in data. But having a lot of data does not automatically produce value. Data alone is not sufficient for making correct decisions or successfully carrying out plans. If a marketing executive, sitting at her desktop computer, can instantly find out how many units of a product she manages sold yesterday, that number alone is of little value. The number's business value increases if it is delivered alongside information about sales over the quarter, the year, and several years, along with the sales targets and whatever is known about the sales performance of competing products.

Larry Prusak and Tom Davenport in *Working Knowledge* state that data is converted into information by adding value to it in a number of ways. Data can be:

- Contextualized: paired with an account of where it came from and the purpose for which it was gathered

- Categorized: organized in terms of units of analysis or key components

- Calculated: analyzed mathematically or statistically

- Corrected: errors have been removed from the data

- Condensed: summarized in a more concise form[1]

Numbers organized in a spreadsheet to reveal a pattern of gains and losses over time are usable information. Inventory records that indicate how quickly merchandise is being purchased and distributed in different regions at different times of the year are usable information. Analyst reports that measure and calculate market trends and present them in the form of executive summaries are usable information—extremely valuable to business leaders who need to make informed decisions quickly.

For data to have value in a business context, it must be packaged and organized so that the recipient can make the most of it. Managers need to ensure that the data they are receiving and the data they are distributing is in a form that can be easily and quickly understood and acted upon. Information management is focused on doing just this—transforming data into a usable format. Much of the last 30 years of business computer use is the story of building applications that translate data into formats that are useful in a business context such as payroll programs, inventory management systems, and customer profile reports.

> ### *ACT on Information*
>
> *Three questions can help you quickly assess whether the information you work with in your organization is information people can ACT upon:*
>
> - *A–Accessible*
>   *Can it be found and sent easily?*
>
> - *C–Contextualized*
>   *Is it formatted and organized in a way that I and others can make use of it?*
>
> - *T–Timely*
>   *Is it current enough so that decisions based on it will have relevance?*

Knowledge

Knowledge is more than an accumulation of bits of information. Knowledge ultimately resides within individuals and is their application of their understanding to a set of information.

Knowledge is information that is first absorbed into and filtered through the beliefs, experiences, capabilities, and judgments of the learner, and then interpreted by that learner, and turned to productive use, action, and decision making. In our musical analogy, knowledge is the score in the hands of a talented musician who turns it into a jazz improvisation. In a business setting, a spreadsheet in the hands of a knowledgeable financial analyst can be converted into investment decisions.

Knowledge in Action

A small company in New England is renowned for making world-class wind instruments. To accelerate production, the company attempted to observe and codify the exact technique used by the master craftsman. His timing and measurements were calibrated and documented. When another craftsperson tried to duplicate the master's technique using his exact measurements, the result was disappointing. The master was incorporating his years of know-how into his instruments and making repeated, subtle adjustments based on the feel of the wood or his intuition about a particular instrument. His methodology (the information) could be captured; his personal know-how could not.

The definition of knowledge as information combined with personal know-how means that, more often than not, knowledge is dynamic, fluid, ever-changing. It is expressed through use—in a moment of making or deciding or teaching or learning or changing. And while knowledge can often be captured and structured, there is much knowledge that is intuitive and mutable. Whereas data and information tend to be fixed points, at least for a period of time, knowledge is often a moving target. And in a world economy where ever-increasing change is the only constant, the ability to combine changing information with evolving know-how is the best competitive advantage.

Knowledge =

Information + Know-How

The Three Classes of Knowledge

Understanding types of knowledge is the key to managing knowledge well. Just as data and information are more valuable when they are managed in keeping with their characteristics, so the knowledge end of the pyramid yields more business value when we see it in terms of three classes of knowledge. Each class of knowledge operates in a distinct way and requires a different set of management practices.

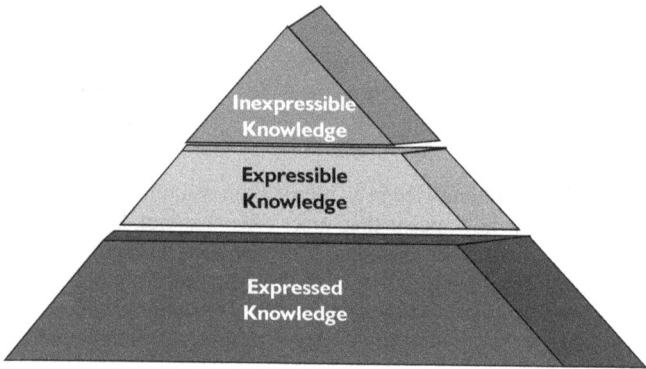

Expressed Knowledge—
What We Know We Know

Expressed knowledge is relatively enduring and unchanging. This is knowledge that can be objectified—extracted from individuals' unique and subjective understanding and fully and clearly expressed in words (or some other medium). A U.S. Geological Survey topographical map of a valley, for example, is a relatively objective expression of "the lay of the land." It captures aspects of the place everyone can agree on and presents them in a format that helps people accomplish a variety of practical goals.

In the same way, the owner's manual for your car contains knowledge, based on research and experience, that embodies best practices for maintaining your car. You can learn when to rotate your tires and change the oil and use this knowledge to your advantage. A travel guide, based on a seasoned traveler's hands-on experience, is knowledge that has been expressed and can now be used by others. In a different medium, a robotic surgical device can be programmed to carry out some kinds of surgical moves. In this instance, knowledge is not only recorded —on the robot's microchips—but also automated.

Expressed knowledge borders closely on information. Terms, measurements, definitions, guidelines, descriptions, and directions are typical elements of documents that express knowledge. Expressed knowledge lends itself to repetition. If a travel guide correctly explains how to get from Boston to New York by train, every person who follows its instructions should, with luck, arrive at Penn Station.

In business, expressed knowledge is captured in documents, databases, and work processes. A company's human resources policy handbook, for example, represents the combined knowledge of human resources staff, other employees, and legal experts, codified and explained for everyday guidance. Most established companies have a vast set of expressed knowledge. New employees, on their first day, encounter expressed company knowledge through orientation programs and literature. For sales and marketing staff, a sales tracking system that retains the records of customer contacts is a vital form of expressed knowledge. In a hospital, the procedure for responding to a Code Blue situation is thoroughly documented. It has also been so well rehearsed that it is part of the operating practices familiar to all personnel. By contrast, startup companies are often too occupied with day-to-day activities to take the time to codify their knowledge. It tends to remain unwritten until a new company reaches a certain size.

Federal Express: Turning Expressed Knowledge into Profit

Before the emergence of the Web, Federal Express developed and implemented an internal, technology-based system for automating shipping, tracking, and invoicing. In 1993, Federal Express started to bring this functionality to the Internet on a Web platform that gave customers access to shipping information 24 hours a day. Customers were able to input their tracking code and trace the route their packages had taken, from point of pick-up to delivery. This level of customer access proved to be a tremendous competitive advantage. Federal Express is able to continually deepen its customer responsiveness by tracking how customers use this website, what they complain about, and what additional features they want.

Expressed knowledge is an important corporate asset. It represents "how we do things here" and what we know we know. It has practical value and profit value. Many professional services and consulting companies have codified their methodologies and have created databases of reusable knowledge assets such as strategic inventories and contract templates. The capture and reuse of these assets ensures consistency across practice areas and improves efficiency.

Managers need to pay attention to what constitutes expressed knowledge in their organizations. They need to review what practices, policies, and learnings are captured and stored in manuals and databases and on websites. Questions such as the following help in effectively managing expressed knowledge:

- Is it current or does it need updating?

- Is it easily accessible?

- Is it organized so that people from different divisions and functions within the organization can use it?

- Is it sufficient without being excessive?
- Can it be leveraged to provide better service to customers?

Expressible Knowledge— What We Know We Know But Haven't Noted

Expressible knowledge is what people in the organization know they know, but they can rarely tell you where to find it in a particular document or process. Expressible knowledge resembles the family secret for making that special holiday cake, handed down from generation to generation—family members just know how to make it even though the recipe has never been written down.

Expressed knowledge comes packaged in enough context or explanation so that someone relatively new can pick it up and make sense of it and use it. Anyone can pick up that travel guide and read it and use it to enhance the value of their next vacation. But not everyone can make Grandma's holiday cake. Expressible knowledge comes without a formal wrapper and depends on the individual to provide sufficient context to understand how to put it to use.

A chemical scientist moving into a new clinical laboratory already understands basic chemistry and laboratory procedures. However, this new lab will have certain protocols and ways of doing things that are different than her previous lab. Some of these new ways will be formally codified in a manual; others will not. She brings with her sufficient background to understand what she experiences, and she learns the new ways through observation, questioning, and instruction. Everyone in the lab knows how work gets done there, and they can correct the new person if she deviates. They can point out shortcuts and describe how to get resources. In the same way, a lead salesperson who has been in charge of a major account for many years has the history of that account etched in her memory. She knows who the key buyers are, what the company's internal landscape looks like, what their business strategy is, and what the potential resource needs will be. If you ask her, she can tell you. However, this invaluable knowledge may not be written down in a form that can easily be shared.

Both these examples illustrate a kind of expressible knowledge we call *Know-What.* It's knowledge, distributed among individuals, about:

- How things work
- How things get done
- What works and what doesn't

It can be documented and codified, but often isn't. People are too busy, or it seems just as easy to ask someone directly.

Another type of expressible knowledge is *Know-Who*. This is knowledge about who's who, about expertise. Know-Who is an extremely valuable form of knowledge. This is particularly true in a knowledge economy in which information changes so quickly that it is often obsolete before it can be documented. When you work at the speed of knowledge, you may not be able to wait for the document; you may need to go to the source—the expert who either created or understands how to use the knowledge. In most companies, you find the source of the knowledge you require by trolling through your personal network. You pick a likely contact and ask, "Do you know anyone who knows anything about . . .?" Eventually, with good contacts and good luck, you gain access to the person with the knowledge you need. This method is familiar to all but can be time-consuming and depends to a high degree on serendipity.

Many companies are beginning to convert this intangible but expressible Know-Who into documented knowledge. They use technology-based expert network systems such as on-line white pages in which people's formal and informal credentials can be searched. In this way you can open a database or a website and search for a particular genre of expertise from among a much broader candidate pool than is normally available to you through your own personal network.

> *Expressible Knowledge:*
> *Know-What*
> *plus*
> *Know-Who*

Expressible knowledge can be written down but it can also be captured in a work process or software system. Federal Express captures its work-flow process in a proprietary technology system. Levi Strauss embeds its production and retail knowledge in a system that enables mass customization—the ability to tailor items to individual customer requirements on a massive scale. Rather than a "one size fits all" approach, Levi Strauss has a "we fit all sizes" approach. The company can then use the customer information it receives to further target markets and be even more responsive.

Managers should be particularly alert to mining for rich deposits of expressible knowledge in their organizations. This form of knowledge, when found and captured, can become a manageable corporate asset. When left unexpressed, this knowledge easily disappears as its possessors move on. This is a particular danger in an economy in which the skilled knowledge worker is an essential and scarce commodity sought by many companies. If she takes her knowledge with her when she leaves, the company loses an asset.

> *Managers should look for opportunities to capture:*
> - *Lessons learned*
> - *Best practices and procedures*
> - *Customer relationship information*
> - *Reusable templates, parts, and methodologies*

Inexpressible Knowledge—
What We Know That Can't Be Noted

Inexpressible knowledge is knowledge that resides inside the mind of the expert. It is knowledge that is mature and insightful. It incorporates measures of that person's intuition, experience, talent, judgment, and expertise. The flute maker's knowledge is largely inexpressible. A conductor's knowledge of how to weave music and musicians together to create a symphony is largely inexpressible. A psychotherapist helping a patient to recover from some past trauma is using inexpressible experience and intuition as part of her treatment.

All of these practitioners have a solid base of theory and learning behind them. Some may be expressed. Much is expressible. However, they all add to the outcome their unique abilities, values, and innate expertise. This is the inexpressible. They may or may not be aware of the extra ingredients they are adding to the mix. And even if they could explain what they are doing, another practitioner could follow the instructions but would still be unable to mimic their effort and achieve the same results.

What Is the Knowledge Economy?

Mrs. Carnegie, they say, wanted a new hat for Easter, so she sent for Paris's most famous chapelier to come to New York and fit her. "And where in the church will you be sitting, Madame?" he inquired, "and what will you be wearing, and what time of day, and what impression would you like to leave?" Finally, he took a crimson ribbon from his bag, fussed it around a plain straw bonnet, tied the bow just so, and put the hat on her head, giving it a forward slant. He held a mirror to her face—Mrs. Carnegie beamed. "Oh, Monsieur, it is perfect! How much do I owe you?" "Five hundred dollars, Madame." She spied him coldly. "Five hundred dollars for a ribbon?" He tugged the ribbon out of the hat, lay it across her forearm and bowed: "Madame," he said, "the ribbon is free."

Civilization Magazine, August-September 2000

In a business context, inexpressible knowledge is priceless. The people who have it are often the "go to" people—those whom others would name as the expert or go to as a reliable or innovative resource. The "alpha" developer who can visualize the way through a knotty problem; the salesperson who is brought in to make the hard close; the human resources manager who is called on to help repair interpersonal damage—these people are using their inexpressible knowledge to solve problems and create possibilities.

These are the people who can be called on to respond rapidly to an urgent business need or a rapidly changing set of circumstances. In a business climate in which rapid change and unpredictability are the norms, existing polices and practices and knowledge bases may not be adequate. It is imperative to have knowledgeable resources to call on who can combine changing information with their expertise to determine the best course of action. They represent the most valuable assets a company competing in a knowledge economy can have.

In fact, increasing this know-how and spreading it widely throughout the organization is one of the most important and most urgent goals for companies. The more expertise is spread and embedded, the more people you have with expertise, the more dynamic, usable knowledge becomes part of the DNA of the organization.

Unlike expressed knowledge, which can be transmitted via documents, and expressible knowledge, which can be found and codified and then transmitted, inexpressible knowledge remains in the mind. The way to extend inexpressible knowledge is through social interaction and dialogue. Creating opportunities for collaboration and exchange builds the pathways for spreading this form of knowledge.

Managers need to foster these opportunities. IBM Research holds symposia periodically for researchers and scientists in various specialty areas. At these face-to-face gatherings, scientists from all over the world meet each other and hear formal presentations. More importantly, they meet each other informally—often in groupings that would not have occurred otherwise. These informal events act as crucibles for bringing out ideas, experiences, and problems, and for catalyzing new possibilities and combinations. One scientist describes a road block she has encountered in her research and another scientist, working on a separate project on another continent, shares how she resolved a similar problem. Both people not only learn about new possibilities, but they create the seeds for future collaboration. They may not have known of each other's existence previously and would have had no way to stumble into each other's work.

Some companies set up their offices so as to foster unplanned encounters and exchanges. Traditional office architecture separates people in offices or cubicles. They meet at scheduled times in large conference rooms. Now many companies are experimenting with more modular architecture, which permits greater fluidity. An e-business consulting company in Boston has designed its space to create opportunities for people to run into each other, overhear conversations, and have informal conversations. People have to walk through common areas to get to their own desks. No one has a permanent desk. Desks change owners as work assignments change. People move to a new area when they have a new project and take their file cabinet with them. In this way, the company hopes to increase the potential for cross-pollination of ideas and possibilities.

A very important way of promoting social networks in organizations is through the use of teams and communities of interest and practice. These organizational forms are essential for getting work done and for enhancing innovation. In distributed, global organizations, both these forms can operate virtually, using technology as their platform for interaction. More will be said about this in a later chapter.

Take a Moment

Take a moment to think about the knowledge requirements of your organization.

- Think about your company's balance of data, information, and knowledge:
  - How does the company record and store the things you need to know or could use if you had access to them? Does the knowledge material you can access come in a form you can easily use or do you have to provide structure, order, and context yourself?

- Think about the accuracy and timeliness of your existing knowledge sources:
  - Does what you can access on databases, on an intranet, or through other means seem "after-the-fact" and hard to apply to what's happening this month, this week, or today? Or is it often quite helpful? Do you get your best information through organized means? Or does it work better to use informal and ad hoc paths to find out what you need?

- Think about what expertise you have within your organization that could be captured and leveraged:
  - What do you do when you need to find an internal expert? Is it easy or difficult to find someone outside the range of your usual work? Do you feel that you and your colleagues have a handle on who knows what in your company? Or does it all seem a little mysterious and hard to unravel?

- Think about ways in which you could extend and sustain informal social networks to increase the overall "knowledge combustion" potential of your organization:
  - Is the culture of your company one that seems receptive to informal gatherings of people with shared interests? Does the technology in place support the easy creation of shared information spaces for people in specific practice areas?

- Is your organization more data-centric, information-centric, or knowledge-centric?
  - In other words, is your company focused on collecting and storing data (like the IRS)? Or does it place a high value on codified ways of doing things and describing things (like an insurance claims office or a printing press)? Or is the expressible and inexpressible knowledge of individuals and teams its most valued asset (like a consulting firm, a software firm, or a university)?

- What are the main expressed knowledge assets in your organization? Do these provide value? Are they being used?
  - Do you have clear guides on processes and procedures? Is useful information on customers accessible? On internal expertise? On key external partners?

- What knowledge exists that could be captured and, if made expressible, would be able to provide significant value?
  - Would information on processes and practices be helpful? On markets? On customers? On competitors? Would you benefit from knowing more about who knows what inside your company? Or from being more in touch with the work of your team and related teams?

Recap

In this chapter, we defined knowledge as a business asset. Like other business assets, it can be acquired, developed, measured, and lost. To manage knowledge, businesses need a systematic way to define and analyze it. We provided a definition of knowledge that fits business situations and a way to analyze its components for business use. We explored three layers of understanding—data, information, and knowledge—each of which is managed in different ways. We also looked at the three forms of knowledge in business—expressed knowledge, expressible knowledge, and inexpressible knowledge—and discussed how businesses make use of each.

Endnote

[1] Bulleted text is quoted from Thomas H. Prusak and Larry Davenport, *Working Knowledge: How Organizations Manage What They Know* (Harvard Business School Press, 1999), 4.

Chapter 3
Managing Knowledge: The Process

Once you've defined your knowledge assets—the ones you have and the ones you need—you will need to manage them. Whether your knowledge assets are in the form of data, information, or knowledge, whether they are *expressed, expressible, or inexpressible,* you will now need to apply certain processes to them to make them usable.

Managing knowledge assets involves three key processes:

1. We *create* them—working with *expressed, expressible,* and *inexpressible* sources.

2. We *distribute* them—making them available in the right places at the right time.

3. We *apply* them. Without this step, your company cannot realize the value of the knowledge that has been created and distributed. Applying knowledge effectively is what enables an organization to succeed, through efficiency, through innovation, or by any other means.

Creating Knowledge

Knowledge has to exist before it can be used. There are several methods for creating knowledge. Knowledge can be created internally through dedicated resources or by fostering an overall climate that supports and sustains emergent knowledge wherever it arises. For example, many companies have well-resourced R&D groups. 3M, a company renowned for innovation, has as a goal in its corporate mission statement that 30 percent of its revenues are to come from products under four years old.

In the 1990s, new sales records of over $15 billion annually were set with 30 percent coming from products under four years old. In 1996 alone, $947 million went into R&D. In fact, 3M files nearly 20,000 patent applications every year, and one in eleven of the company's 70,000 employees works for R&D. These corporate values, coupled with a culture and a system that support creativity and innovation, have contributed greatly to 3M's reputation as a leading-edge, creative company.

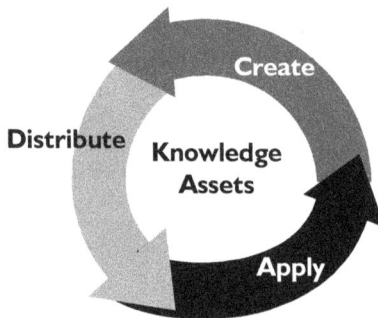

Create

Distribute | Knowledge Assets

Apply

Today, Nokia is the world's leading maker of mobile telephones. Of the 165 million phones sold in 1998, 41 million were Nokia phones. Nokia has achieved its current success by redesigning its innovation process and concentrating its business on mobile phones and networks. Nokia's R&D engineers work in closely knit teams with suppliers, production staff, and marketing people. In some instances, Nokia has brought a new product to market in as little as six weeks.[1]

Knowledge can also be acquired or bought. The rate at which companies are acquiring other companies or merging with their past competitors is dazzling. In 1995, IBM bought Lotus for $3.5 billion, which was many times Lotus' book valuation. IBM was purchasing Lotus' expertise in the Notes software domain to fold this missing ingredient into its own portfolio of offerings. More recently, Hewlett-Packard announced its intention to buy a consulting branch of PricewaterhouseCoopers to augment its own knowledge and expertise for providing complex IT and Internet solutions to business. Many companies also use the services of consultants to add to their expertise base or to fill in holes in their internal competencies.

Knowledge can also be generated through social networks. When knowledgeable people connect with other knowledgeable people, new ideas emerge. These networks can exist within the boundaries of the organization or can extend beyond to link companies to companies, to customers, to research institutions, to analyst groups. Conferences, colloquia, roundtables, seminars, and other professional meetings are formal opportunities to gather and exchange knowledge—and are valued as much for informal, unscripted social exchanges as for what's on the program. Many universities sponsor corporate consortiums to target their own research initiatives and to provide companies with cutting-edge research and an opportunity to interact with knowledgeable colleagues. High-tech companies locate in places like Silicon Valley, Silicon Alley, the North Carolina Research Triangle, and Route 128/Boston because they benefit from being near other companies full of people who excel at and are passionate about similar fields. In the same way, oil and chemical companies cluster around places like Houston and Baton Rouge.

Distributing Knowledge

Distributing knowledge is the process that usually attracts the most attention. Perhaps this is because technology plays a clear and central role in knowledge distribution. Creating and applying knowledge, on the other hand, depend more on social interactions and are, therefore, more complex—and more difficult to measure.

Locating Knowledge. Distribution processes are concerned with finding, packaging, and delivering the right set of data, information, and knowledge to the right people at the right time. The first step is locating the material, either inside or outside the company. It is important to remember that knowledge can reside in many places and take many forms. To find what you want, you must first find out where it lives. Knowledge can be kept in:

- *Places*—recorded in an existing document or database

- *Processes*—embedded in a known work process

- *People*—known to an identified individual

- *Pieces*—distributed in parts among several people or processes (as in a value chain)

How you extract the knowledge will depend largely on where it comes from and what shape it is in. If it is an existing document, you may be able to search for it using keywords. Search technology, information libraries, and news feeds are useful tools for finding recorded or documented knowledge. Many companies collect the documented knowledge they need—from the vast outpouring we mentioned in Chapter 2— by employing information specialists. These people (sometimes called "cybrarians" these days) often have backgrounds in library science or information resources.

If it is embedded in a work process, you may need to take the process apart, analyze it, and extract the pieces that apply to your situation. Knowledge located in processes, persons, or pieces may end up in a technologically searchable place. But much of it is gathered by people, from people, using "people" skills: networking, asking, listening, and asking some more.

Organizing Knowledge. Once you find useful data, information, or knowledge, you need to be sure it is in the right form to be transferred to new contexts. One common mistake is to take a process or best practice that works wonders in one division or region and try to apply it somewhere else. If you work in a company that has major operations on both sides of the Atlantic, you may be familiar with how "global" initiatives that seem perfect for one continent get sent back from the other riddled with objections and criticisms. If proposed knowledge processes are to get past these kinds of problems, careful attention must be paid to regional, cultural, and functional differences.

Business is full of situations in which information that is useful in one context needs reworking to be useful in others. For example, the information a product development group puts together about a new product's specifications is perfectly suited to communications among themselves and with potential suppliers, subcontractors, manufacturers, and other technical partners. Within this mass of information, the marketing department can also find what it needs to market the product. However, for development specs to become marketing material, they must be recast in a language and format better suited to marketing needs.

Repackaging or organizing knowledge is a science unto itself. Some of the tools used in organizing knowledge include classification systems, inventories, taxonomies, summaries, and maps that show interrelationships between clusters of knowledge. The way the company organizes its knowledge is pivotal in enabling employees to find what they need when they need it. Too much structure makes the system hard to use and fragments information too much for business purposes. Not enough structure makes it difficult to navigate to a level of detail where findings are relevant and their quantity is manageable.

Take, for example, a contact management system that contains information about key customers, vendors, partners, and others.

If it is structured too simplistically in a database organized purely by regions such as Northeast, Southeast, Midwest, Southwest, West Coast, and Northwest, it might have tens of thousands of entries in Northeast alone. If it is overly structured, users would have to dig down (and sometimes backtrack) through too many layers of classification before arriving at useful information. Similarly, if a discussion database for a newly forming community dedicated to innovation has hundreds of categories, the sheer number of categories will frustrate users by making information hard to find.

Delivering Knowledge. Once knowledge has been found and packaged, it must be delivered. The delivery mechanism can either push knowledge to users or let them pull it in. "Push technologies" send information to you, such as daily news feeds and email. With some, you set up your interest parameters and the technology pushes information that fits your requirements to you. "Pull technologies" are those in which you initiate a request or a search. Search engines on the Internet or in company intranets are prime examples of pull technologies.

An effective knowledge distribution system uses both push and pull technologies. To get the balance right for employees, companies need to determine their information and delivery needs. Information pushed in excess or at the wrong time causes information overload. The need to pull information will soon frustrate and tire the searcher. The key is to discern which information needs are more constant and predictable and can be pushed (such as a daily accounting of the company financials), and which information needs are more complex or idiosyncratic and should be made available through easily accessed pull technology.

Applying Knowledge

Once knowledge is found and distributed, it needs to be applied for its value to be realized. This is perhaps the knowledge management process that has the largest social and behavioral component. Application requires that people be motivated to produce and perform in the right direction. That is a sociological imperative, not a technological one.

Knowledge must be applied in the service of company goals and objectives. For this to occur, first and foremost, employees need to understand those goals and objectives, at the corporate level and at the level of their own work unit. The application engine of any company is its people, organized into individuals, teams, task forces, communities, and project groups. Each of these units needs to be:

- Clear and motivated about its purpose

- Able to find the knowledge it needs to achieve its objectives

- Able to put that knowledge to use in a work environment that suits the unit's work needs

---

Global Knowledge Management

AXA, a French insurer with $605 billion in assets under management, wants everyone on its international teams to have access to the best ideas in the company—whoever has them and wherever they may be. AXA has established a process and implemented technology for sharing research that would network local fund managers with domestic and industry-sector analysts. This is a first step toward building a globally integrated investment process, using knowledge management approaches and technologies.[2]

49

Technology can play a key part in creating that suitable work environment. But the technology needs to be suited to the work. Today, people rely heavily on e-mail and the phone to do their jobs—and for knowledge exchange. However, the phone doesn't leave a record, so there's no documentation of what was shared. E-mail works person-to-person, but tends to break down when teams of a dozen or more people try to discuss strategy or when three teams are trying to coordinate their efforts. The technology is simply not robust enough to handle the load efficiently. People have inboxes and "sent mail" boxes with hundreds of messages they dare not throw away and don't have time to sort efficiently. Executive teams can't function on this basis. They need tools such as web-based project spaces with virtual team rooms, shared libraries, and expertise-finding systems. These tools are beginning to emerge now.

But technology alone is not the answer. Implementing knowledge management technologies without ensuring that your staff is clear about your company's overall goals and how knowledge technology can help achieve those goals will lead to disappointing returns on your technology investment.

Take a Moment

Let's consider how knowledge management processes happen in your organization. Questions such as the following can help you identify how knowledge management is being conducted and what is and isn't working.

- *How is new knowledge generally created in your organization? Is this sufficient to maintain the right level of innovation?*

- *Are you finding the knowledge you need to do your job? If not, why not?*

- *Is too much information being pushed at you?*

- *Do you have enough direction to be able to put the knowledge to good use?*

- *Are you and your group working in a space that is matched to the requirements of your work?*

- *Is knowledge distribution getting the lion's share of attention, while efforts to create and apply knowledge are ignored?*

Knowledge Users: The Vital Link

In some ways, knowledge isn't really knowledge until the user makes it so. The user must be able to understand the knowledge, in a meaningful context, and be able to put it to use. That's why keeping the user—the knowledge customer—in mind is important in planning how to manage knowledge assets. Each customer may have different requirements for content, packaging, and delivery.

By knowledge user, we mean both individuals and groups. Users of knowledge management systems include:

- Individuals–any employee

- Teams—focused on a task or a project, such as researching a disease, launching a product, or selling in a new region

- Communities—drawn together by an interest, a specialty, a shared area of knowledge

- Organizations—formed around a purpose and encompassing many interests, specialties, and functions that contribute to achieving that purpose

Individuals and Teams. The individual and the team tend to be focused on a very specific goal, task, or project, to which they bring a specialized understanding. They need knowledge delivered in an easy-to-use form that will help them progress.

A benefits manager in Human Resources needs extensive current knowledge in her area: details of the company's current policies, how they benchmark against industry standards, who to contact for further guidance on complex issues. An executive needs regular updates—summaries, not blow-by-blow accounts— about a key product initiative.

A product development team working to deliver a component of a large system will need to know about matters such as specifications, time frames, tool kits, and product features. The team and its members will need to have knowledge that will help them meet their objectives. In addition, they may need and want broader knowledge about impending business issues, company strategy, emerging technology trends, and related fields.

Communities and Organizations. The organization as a whole and its communities of practice (more will be said about communities later) are not only larger, but also less focused and clearly defined than individuals and teams. Individuals and teams produce a clear set of deliverables. Communities and organizations are dedicated to broader interests, goals, and objectives. As a result, their knowledge needs are harder to define and tend to change more rapidly. The company can make knowledge of general interest and use available broadly, and have systems in place for channeling more focused knowledge to particular communities. The knowledge management community at Lotus Development/IBM is a loose affiliation of employees working on many different aspects of knowledge management, including advanced technology, marketing, taxonomies, expertise networks, knowledge strategy, communities, and other areas. There are many databases and newsfeeds with pertinent information available to either all or some members of this broad community.

Many of the major oil companies have moved quickly to develop communities of practice. and specialist networks. Oil companies conduct exploration activities all around the globe. Providing many ways to access scientific and technical expertise on topics like drilling, geology, and geophysics from anywhere in the company helps teams solve often-daunting technical problems faster. Enterprise Oil, for example, uses virtual discussion groups to promote dialogue that is often launched in person at internal conferences and community-of-practice meetings. Royal Dutch/Shell has cultivated a series of specialist networks, supported by the company's Learning Centre and corporate intranet.[3]

Take a Moment

A few key questions can help focus your efforts to understand and meet the needs of knowledge users in your organization:

1. Are their knowledge needs task-specific and/or broader?

2. Are their knowledge needs predictable over a period of time or are they more changeable?

3. Can they understand specialized knowledge or does it need to be packaged with more explanation?

4. Do they want full text or a summary? Would they prefer the knowledge to be pushed to them? Or would they rather pull it in?

Recap

In this chapter, we described the processes used to manage knowledge assets—processes for creating, distributing, and applying knowledge.

- Knowledge creation can happen inside or outside the organization. It can be developed or acquired.

- Knowledge distribution requires finding it, organizing and packaging it, determining whether to push it to individuals or let them pull it toward themselves, and pushing or pulling in a timely way.

- Knowledge application means converting knowledge into results, outputs, and successes that align with strategy and build value for the company.

Finally, applying knowledge means understanding its users, or customers—individuals, teams, communities, and organizations—and offering them the knowledge they need in the manner they prefer. Keep in mind that while it is tempting to lavish effort on technology for knowledge distribution, your efforts should also fully emphasize knowledge creation and application processes.

Endnotes

[1] Steven Silberman, "Just Say Nokia," *Wired*, September 1999; Ronald S. Jonash and Tom Sommerlatte, "The Innovation Premium: Capturing the Value of Creativity," *Prism* (Arthur D. Little, Inc.), Third Quarter 1999.

[2] Dorothy Yu, "Seize the Knowledge Advantage: Use What You Know to Invent What You Need," *Perspectives* (Pricewaterhouse Coopers LLP), Issue 1, 2000.

[3] Nick Milton, "Refined Technique: Why Are the Oil Companies So Far Ahead in Knowledge Management?" *Knowledge Management Magazine* (UK), October 23, 2000 (on-line).

Chapter 4
Making the Connection:
Knowledge Management and
Organizational Learning

In our exploration of the three main forms of knowledge in Chapter 2, we took a look at the specific tactics that can capture each form of knowledge for your organization. Then, in Chapter 3, we showed you, in more detail, how organizations can create, distribute, and apply knowledge. Along the way, we mentioned the need to keep knowledge management efforts linked to strategy and adapted to your organization's culture and core needs.

In this chapter, we introduce a model that helps you focus your knowledge management efforts on building the core competencies that make your company the best in the world at what it does. This focus puts knowledge management at the service of your strategy. And it explicitly links knowledge management with organizational learning.

Let's look at this another way. Today, almost every company's strategic plans involve moving forward into new areas—businesses, markets, regions, technologies—where new skills will be needed. In addition, sources of information, and the information itself, keep changing. The faster a company's people can gain the skills and competencies they need to keep up with the information deluge while taking the company forward, the better the chance that the company will meet its strategic goals. Therefore, the company's collective ability to absorb and sort information and learn—its capacity for organizational learning—is a major factor in its chances of success. Knowledge management is the systematic use of processes that enhance organizational learning. The main purpose of knowledge management is to help companies learn and expand the core competencies—the know-how—they need to carry out their strategies and be the best at what they do.

The RICE Model: Responsiveness, Innovation, Competency, Efficiency

Know-how in your organization is built around four areas of action: responsiveness, innovation, competency, and efficiency. These four areas, which we call the RICE model, cover all of the different ways in which you can use knowledge to help your company succeed. *Responsiveness* concerns how your company takes in vital information from its surroundings: its customers, competitors, suppliers, and others who affect—and are affected by—your company's performance. *Innovation* concerns how your company uses ideas and information to change what it does and how it does it. *Competency* concerns the skills your people and teams need to deliver products and services. *Efficiency* concerns how well your processes for product and service delivery work.[1]

Part of developing a good knowledge strategy is concentrating on the areas that suit your company's business proposition and objectives. For example, if your company is in a business in which being able to consistently deliver the same high-quality products and services at a competitive price is the path to success, then you are likely to focus on *applying* knowledge to improve the competency of your people and the efficiency of your processes. You will be making the most of your current resources and knowledge assets. Total Quality Management systems are an example of a way to efficiently reuse knowledge to improve processes.

The RICE Model for Knowledge Management

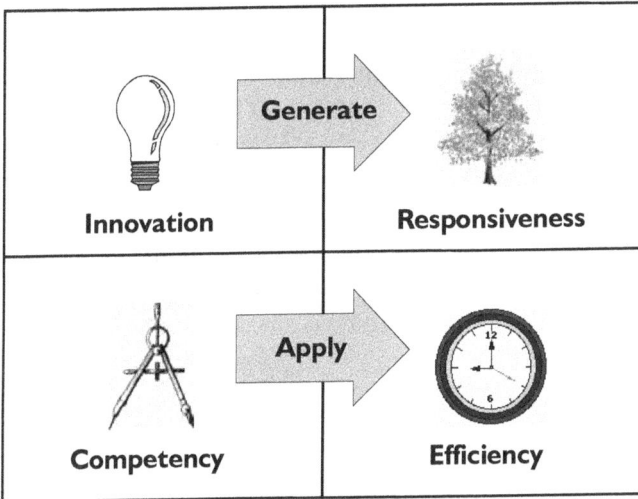

On the other hand, if your company is in a business in which developing and delivering new products and services that reshape markets or create entirely new ones lead to success, then you are likely to focus on *generating* knowledge by hearing what the marketplace is saying—and enabling your employees to communicate with each other—and using that knowledge to innovate.

Most companies, of course, must do both kinds of knowledge management to thrive. They have current products and services to maintain in the marketplace, and they are developing the next generation of offerings to build a position in tomorrow's marketplace. The purpose of the RICE model is not to assign a particular approach, but to help you define the key pieces of a knowledge strategy, assess where you have strengths or weaknesses, and focus on what will help your company the most.

Competency and Efficiency

From Individual Competency to Organizational Efficiency.
Organizational learning builds organizational knowledge. But
all learning, all knowledge, all know-how, starts in and resides
with individuals. People in organizations often act collectively,
but they learn based on their own interests, aptitudes, and
motivators—and based on what they believe will protect or
improve their standing in the organization. Ideally, they are also
motivated to learn the competencies that help the organization
most. But we can't always count on that to happen automatically.

Starting with Competency. The first stage in building the
knowledge of the organization is to hire people who already
have the needed skills. The hiring process begins with identifying
the needed knowledge and skills and then builds a recruiting,
marketing, and retention program that identifies and attracts the
right people with the right skills (see *Manager's Pocket Guide to
Employee Selection and Retention*).

The second stage in building individual competency is managing
"time to talent." How quickly can an organization take novices or
new employees and turn their talent into activity that adds value
to the firm? There are two approaches to improving time to talent:

- Formal training programs
- Communities of practice

Formal training programs focus on giving people the tools they
need to learn what they need just then (just-in-time learning) or
what they might need sometime (just-in-case learning). School-
like training—in a group, with a leader, at a specific time and
place—still plays a large role in training. More and more,
however, companies are using on-line, on-demand forms of
training that can be tailored much more precisely to individual
needs. Beyond that, through distance learning or e-learning
capabilities, faculty members and other experts become available

as on-line consultants to help practitioners solve real problems. The problems and their solutions can then be integrated into the company's knowledge base to share the learning more broadly and help employees bring the best approaches to bear on real issues.

Communities of practice are a powerful way to build organizational learning. Research shows that people learn as much as 70 percent of what they need to know to do their jobs from interactions with colleagues. As communities of practice help increase individual competency, they also serve as a place to cultivate and expand the codified knowledge of the organization.

Moving to Efficiency. Knowledge circulates in a company in a very dynamic way—moving, often erratically and unpredictably, to individuals, to teams, to communities, and to knowledge bases—and changing along the way. Codifying knowledge is a key way of circulating it more broadly and making it usable throughout the organization.

Codification, where possible, becomes very important in the cycle. By codifying individual, team, and community know-how and making it reusable, companies can improve the overall efficiency of the organization. Efficiency, in other words, reflects a company's ability to turn individual learning, knowledge, and ability about getting things done into repeatable processes many people can follow with good results.

The process of building organizational efficiency and competency is also the process of building organizational memory. Memory allows us to "know what we know" and supports the efficient use of processes and practices that have already been used successfully. Taking new learning and codifying it into organizational memory is an ongoing process. As we discussed in Chapter 2, the rapid pace of change requires that new processes and practices be invented to respond to market and environmental demands. By intentionally linking the learning that takes place as work gets done into a codified process, organizations can increase the chances that everyone in an organization will learn from a particular experience and that organizational processes are being redefined to meet current needs.

The Dynamic Movement of Knowledge Leading to Profit

A company researcher went to a conference on synthetic fibers. Soon after he returned, he had lunch with a group of colleagues and described an interesting presentation on a new process developed by an Asian firm. One of the other people at the lunch happened to refer to the presentation in an e-mail to a group of people in the company. By chance, one of the recipients of the e-mail message sat next to a senior executive on a flight and mentioned the new process. The senior executive thought the idea was promising and described it at the meeting he was traveling to, which happened to be about finding new business opportunities. Based on a report he wrote on the idea, the firm sent a delegation to the Asian firm to look at the process more closely. They liked what they saw. The manufacturer eventually licensed the process and used it to develop a profitable new product line.

Conference Board Proceedings, April 1997

Xerox's Project Eureka is an example of systematically building on the knowledge shared and developed within communities of practice. Anthropologist Julian Orr studied the behavior of Xerox repair representatives. He noted that the reps frequently met together to have coffee or lunch. At these social meetings, they asked questions about work, discussed changes in work processes or in the machines they repaired, and shared problem-solving approaches that worked. These social encounters, and the sharing of what worked and what did not, clearly nurtured and developed the skills of individual repair representatives. Some reps emerged as "master problem-solvers," well known throughout Xerox for their competency.

To leverage the learning that was taking place within these local communities of repair representatives, Xerox launched Project Eureka. Eureka is a shared database of tips and best practices, reviewed by experienced repair technicians and product specialists. As John Seely Brown and Paul Duguid report in *Harvard Business Review*, technicians' use of these tips and best practices have saved the corporation an estimated $100 million. For example, an engineer in Brazil was about to replace a problematic high-end color machine for a disgruntled customer (at a cost of $40,000). Experimenting with a prototype of Eureka, he found a tip from a Montreal technician that led him to replace a defective 50-cent fuse instead.[2]

Innovation and Responsiveness

From Enhanced Responsiveness to Sustainable Innovation.
Innovations are responses to challenging problems or even desperate situations. Creativity emerges when the existing solutions no longer serve their purpose and new responses are called for. For example, the digital revolution that is turning the business world inside out traces some of its technological roots to the struggle to prevail in World War II and the Cold War. As scientists and mathematicians on both sides searched for ways to automate the massive calculations required to break enemy ciphers and determine ballistic missile trajectories, they developed new technologies that became the seedbed for today's advances. In a period of crisis, a century's worth of abstruse theoretical work in mathematics was integrated into the foundations of a technological revolution that just keeps getting bigger.

In the business world, responsiveness is about listening to customers and reading signals from the marketplace. It's an area in which many companies tend to be caught in permanent "adhocracy"—partly because they haven't used knowledge management to systematically scan for market signals and then make systematic sense of the signals or compare notes from responses in different parts of the company. Faced with a particular customer need or change in the market, staff try to move quickly to develop a customized solution. But often the learning doesn't become institutionalized. Each crisis gets a customized solution, when it might be possible to apply previous solutions.

How can knowledge management enhance responsiveness and make it more efficient? Through effective responsiveness systems, customer needs or problems are brought to the attention of the business—not just to individuals who deal with customers. When these needs become visible, they can be solved. Moreover, the results can be shared and the solution can become part of the service or product. In some instances, it can become a new product or service.

Just as knowledge management can better align responsiveness with your customer interests and your business strategy and objectives, it can also support and strengthen the innovation process. In many companies, a lack of ideas is not what's hindering innovation. It's implementing the ones that have the most promise. This, too, requires a knowledge management process—a systematic way to evolve and implement innovation. To bring ideas to fruition, a company needs an organized way to identify them, develop them (in part through collaborative discussion), sort through and pick the best ones, and then bring the best people together to pilot and implement them.

Take a Moment

Designing a Knowledge Management Strategy

The following questions can help in developing an integrated strategy for knowledge management:

1. Where is the business heading?
2. What kinds of information do we need to move forward?
3. Where does that information reside and how is it renewed?
4. What competencies do we need in our workforce to be able to apply that information?
5. What collaborative structures, processes, roles, and incentives do we need to support the renewal and application of knowledge?
6. What measures would help us track progress?
7. What are our current basic cultural assumptions and are they the ones we need to support ongoing learning?

Building a Knowledge Culture

For knowledge management to have its intended impact, the role of culture must be understood and managed. Culture is both obvious and subtle. It is easy to identify and describe the overall cultural flavor of a company like IBM or Microsoft. It is evident in regulations, institutional processes, technology, work ethic, and personnel practices. However, there are more subtle cultural undercurrents that exist within each division and within each work group that can influence the successful absorption of new ideas and new ways of working. The beliefs, values, behaviors, norms, and roles of a group are critical to the way they integrate and use new knowledge. And what makes this level of culture even more tricky is that often there is a disparity between how people say they behave and the way they actually do. A group

63

may claim that they share information freely while in reality the information is shared only within an inner clique. Or a group may appear eager to adapt a new decision system, but the leader, wanting to retain control over decision making, indirectly obstructs the effort.

Many organizations have suffered the misfortune of investing in new technology, only to find that the swift integration and efficiency enhancement that they hoped for has been thwarted. The problem in many instances is not the technology itself. Instead, elements within the company are resisting the cultural changes the technology enables. A classic example: When voice mail was first introduced at a major global professional services firm, one senior partner wasn't ready to take on the management of his own phone traffic. Instead, he asked his administrative assistant to listen to all of his voice mail messages (as many as 30 at a time) every morning and evening and provide him with a transcript. Instead of realizing the labor- and time-saving potential of voice mail, he managed to make it more laborious than the old system—since his assistant was still answering his phone and writing down messages all day.

More broadly, the business intention of knowledge management tools is often to accelerate decision making by providing unlimited (or vastly expanded) information at all levels. But in cultures that believe that information is power and that those who guard the most information have the most power, information-guarding habits will win out over the new technology—unless that belief is brought to the surface and managed.

In our work with companies focused on learning and innovation, we see three essential cultural components for developing a knowledge management system:

- Openness around information sharing
- Leadership accountability for supporting and modeling collaboration and empowerment
- A core function linked to business strategy

Elements of a Learning Organization

In "The Learning Organization: Managing Knowledge for Business Success," a 1996 study conducted by the Economist Intelligence Unit and IBM, 400 senior executives and managers were surveyed on their perceptions of the elements that go into building a learning culture. They identified 11 key elements:

1. *Articulation and continual reinforcement of values and goals that go beyond profits*
2. *Learning or innovation as a corporate goal*
3. *Individual performance measurement systems that identify specific learning objectives*
4. *Rewards and compensations that take learning achievements and collaborative behaviors into consideration*
5. *Structures and routine work activities that encourage the sharing of ideas*
6. *Strong cultivation of corporate history and traditions*
7. *Trust and frequent communication between upper management and all other levels*
8. *Physical work environments that promote teamwork and the spontaneous flow of ideas*
9. *Routine meetings that include discussions of the company's values*
10. *Compatibility with corporate values included as a factor in recruiting and hiring*
11. *Organization of people into smaller work groups to encourage entrepreneurialism*

The study distinguishes those companies that have learning embedded in their culture from those that must build it incrementally. An example of a learning culture is 3M, whose culture is characterized by a deep respect for the individual, support for innovation and initiative, and a tolerance of mistakes, including the legendary mistake that led to the creation of Scotch tape.

Information Sharing. Music may be the food of love, but information is the food of learning. Unless a culture permits and supports open access to information, knowledge management will have a hard time taking root. When information is restricted and pathways blocked, researchers can't find key pieces of the puzzles they are solving—and eventually they learn to stop looking. When workers are free to forage in whatever fields they think might be fruitful, encountering new possibilities and collaborating with other searchers as they proceed, accelerated learning and just-in-time learning happen. One success tends to encourage others, opening the doors to information-sharing, collaboration, and even wider learning.

Leadership. In a study conducted by the Economist Intelligence Unit and IBM (see box), 60 percent of respondents stated that "top management leadership by example" is the most important element in building a learning culture. Leaders of learning organizations possess, as one of their core assumptions, a commitment to valuing knowledge and collaboration. They believe these things contribute powerfully to corporate success. They show their commitment both in their behavior and in how they dedicate resources. If there is a discrepancy between what leaders say they support and what they do, intentional or not, the organization will follow what they do rather than what they say.

Paul O'Neill, the CEO of Alcoa from 1987 to 2000, showed his commitment to the power of information, collaboration, and learning with his intense involvement in the design of Alcoa's new headquarters building in Pittsburgh. O'Neill had spent years gathering information about how buildings affect the way people work. He worked with a Pittsburgh architect to create a working environment that would support his learning-driven management strategy. At Alcoa's former headquarters, a 30-story building with banks of elevators, departments were sequestered on different floors and staff behind doors. The new building's interior spaces follow an open floor plan. Everyone, including the company's most senior management, has virtually identical workstations that alternate with plentiful informal meeting areas. Larger open spaces and the total layout (including escalators rather than elevators) encourage chance meetings and a much greater awareness of who is who and what they do than is possible in a traditional office building. O'Neill himself and his senior leadership team occupied workstations just like everyone else. "I see more people now by accident than I ever did on purpose because it's a natural consequence of the way we have organized the flow," he told a reporter for the *New York Times* in 1998.[3]

Companies who are very serious about building a learning culture demonstrate their intent where it will show the most—in their compensation systems. 3M, for example, promotes ongoing innovation by tying senior compensation to the percentage of sales that comes from new products.

Core Function. To be effective, knowledge management must be a core business function in the culture like marketing, finance, human resources, or any other function. As a core function, it is aligned with the company's objectives, it is broadly implemented, and it has appropriate resources. The function's performance is measured against defined performance targets and is evaluated and reshaped according to how it meets those targets.

A leading consulting firm has organized its knowledge management system around its primary communities of practice and has established formal processes for collecting best practices. The company has set up three levels of consultants to support the capturing, screening, and selecting of information. The partner responsible for each industry area acts as a knowledge sponsor outlining the big picture. With that direction, a knowledge integrator defines the content for each practice area. Herman Miller, a furniture design and manufacturing company, has 20 full- and part-time learning coaches assigned to functional business areas to identify learning needs and provide coaching.

Nokia, a global telecommunications company, has instituted team-based technology to support corporate strategy planning and conducts team-based executive development.

Take a Moment

Assessing Your Organization's Readiness to Become a Learning Organization

Before you invest time, effort, and resources in building a learning organization supported by knowledge management, it helps to know how ready your organization is—how prepared the culture is for using learning as a business asset. The following questionnaire can help you identify strengths that will support the effort, as well as roadblocks that could slow it down.

		Strongly Agree				Strongly Disagree
1.	Individuals are given incentives to work together and share information.	1	2	3	4	5
2.	Cross-functional and team information and knowledge sharing is encouraged.	1	2	3	4	5
3.	Individuals are willing to take the time to provide information to others when asked.	1	2	3	4	5
4.	Individuals' ideas and contributions are generally valued by the organization.	1	2	3	4	5
5.	The organization encourages individuals to learn and grow with help from their peers and provides methods for them to do so.	1	2	3	4	5
6.	The organization is willing to adopt practices and ideas that are created outside its bounds.	1	2	3	4	5

(continued on next page)

Assessing Your Organization's Readiness to Become a Learning Organization *(concluded)*

		Strongly Agree				Strongly Disagree
7.	Management clearly recognizes the need for knowledge management.	I	2	3	4	5
8.	Individuals within the organization understand the need for knowledge management.	I	2	3	4	5
9.	The knowledge management project is linked to the overall organizational goals and strategy.	I	2	3	4	5
10.	The organization has a good history of successfully implementing change initiatives.	I	2	3	4	5
11.	Management is willing to try new tools and methods.	I	2	3	4	5
12.	There is a pool of potential internal sponsors for knowledge management.	I	2	3	4	5
13.	These potential sponsors are willing to provide active leadership and devote time to the initiative.	I	2	3	4	5
14.	They understand what is required for active change.	I	2	3	4	5
15.	They have a significant stake in the success of the initiative.	I	2	3	4	5
16.	They have a visible and fairly senior role in the organization and would be project "champions."	I	2	3	4	5

If you agree strongly that many of these statements describe your organization or your part of your organization, then your business culture is likely to support organizational learning.

Source: "Communities of Practice: The Business Value" (Cambridge, Massachusetts: Lotus Development Corporation, 2000).

Recap

In this chapter, we introduced a model that helps you focus knowledge management efforts on building the core competencies that make your company the best in the world at what it does. We emphasized how knowledge management is the systematic use of processes that enhance organizational learning—which is what builds core competencies. We introduced the RICE model—responsiveness, innovation, competencies, efficiency—as a way to structure and focus how you develop knowledge management in your organization, keeping it linked to strategy and business value. We discussed how learning begins with individuals, as they acquire competencies, and spreads into the organization to promote efficiency—the ability to do things right over and over again. We explored how a knowledge management approach can bring structure and results to responsiveness—the process of taking in information from customers, markets, and other key stakeholders—and to innovation—the process of developing new products and services that meet and anticipate customer needs and wants. Finally, we examined the key role culture plays in supporting knowledge management.

Endnotes

[1] The RICE model was created by the authors and other Lotus colleagues through research at Lotus.

[2] John Seely Brown and Paul Duguid, "How to Capture Knowledge Without Killing It," *Harvard Business Review*, May–June 2000, 73-80. Reprint #R00309.

[3] Trish Hall, "And the Walls Came Tumbling Down," *New York Times Sunday Magazine*, December 13, 1998.

Chapter 5
Getting Started and Going Forward

In this chapter, we show you how to launch a knowledge management initiative. We will focus on two key areas:

- Getting started
- Going forward

The goal of knowledge management is not to pursue knowledge for its own sake or to be seduced by technology. Rather, companies manage knowledge to enhance their unique competitive advantage by increasing their overall know-how—the core competencies that help them do the things they do better than any other company. To expand know-how, you need to capture knowledge in both its explicit and tacit forms. You need to develop both information technology and the social relationships through which people learn much of what they learn at work.

If your company is the world leader in a niche market, providing widgets that extend the life expectancy of the leading brand of hearing aid, then your core competencies and strategies will center on defining and reaching buyers of that specific product and never losing sight of their specific needs. It would be unnecessary to evolve a knowledge management strategy focused on new product development. But it might be highly useful to have your knowledge management strategy include a way for the sales and distribution forces to be better aligned in sharing information about expected deals, customer ordering cycles, and customer product development activities.

> *"Core competencies are not products or those things we do relatively well; they are those activities—usually intellectually based service activities or systems—that the company performs better than any other company. They are the set of skills and systems that a company does at 'best in world' levels and through which a company creates uniquely high value for customers."*
>
> James Brian Quinn, Professor Emeritus at the Amos Tuck School of Management at Dartmouth College[1]

If, on the other hand, your company's success tends to ride on the freshness of its ideas and products, the knowledge you nurture centers around new product development. By getting back to offering personal computers that look and "feel" different, Apple revived its fortunes and its brand with the iMac and the iBook computers. For years, Gillette's fortunes have ridden upon new generations of razors that work better than their predecessors. For all the jokes Viagra has spawned, it has spawned even more profits for Pfizer—an excellent return on the R&D investment in this remedy. Getting the ideas right, keeping schedules tight, and meeting or exceeding expectations, not only for innovation, but also for quality and availability, become your core competencies. Knowledge activities should focus on building know-how in those areas.

As we discuss how to get started, we will provide you with a process, a model, and a set of questions to help you stay on a strategic track and avoid veering off into the deep technology woods. As we discuss how to implement a knowledge management initiative, we will offer you best practices and guidelines.

Getting Started

Imagine that you are the newly appointed Vice President of Human Resources in a global Fortune 500 consumer products company. Your senior executive team has decided that better management of its knowledge resources will yield benefits such as closer ties to the customer and greater responsiveness to changing market requirements. The team has made knowledge management one of its top 10 corporate initiatives. They have given you a mandate: institute knowledge management initiatives throughout your organization. Where do you begin?

You have heard about decision support systems, information portals, customer relationship management systems, partner relationship management systems, document management systems, knowledge mapping, on-line learning, virtual teaming—the list grows longer every day. And under the pressure of your corporate mandate, it is tempting to jump into action and install something you can point to. However, in our experience, jumping without the necessary strategic due diligence proves to be expensive and counterproductive. Success with knowledge management demands not only the right fit between technology or process and the business need, but also an implementation process that wins buy-in, not resistance.

Knowledge Management Landscape. You have to focus and choose your path. The RICE model, described in the previous chapter, helps focus thinking on your company's core competencies and strategic growth areas. Using it, you can determine whether your company needs to develop, maintain, or expand strength in the areas of:

- Responsiveness to the market
- Innovation of new products and services
- Competency of your skill base
- Efficiency of work processes

Now, building on the RICE model, we will offer you a more detailed framework and diagnostic questions from which you can begin to tailor practical knowledge management initiatives for your organization. The following framework illustrates the knowledge management landscape within which you can map your own unique situation. Each element of this framework defines solutions related to the areas of the RICE model—responsiveness, innovation, competency, and efficiency.

We have used our model with many companies to help them imagine what is possible. No company can or should implement every element of the model. Its purpose is to open up possibilities, which your company can then assess on its reality meter using strategic priorities, cultural determinants, and fiscal constraints.

As we explore this model, remember that in the real world nothing is as compact and delineated as it can appear on paper. The edges of each area will inevitably blur and run into other areas. You should not think of this as a jigsaw puzzle where each piece has its neat place. Rather, think of it as a dynamic, moving montage—with overlap, change, and redirection happening as market and internal strategy dictates.

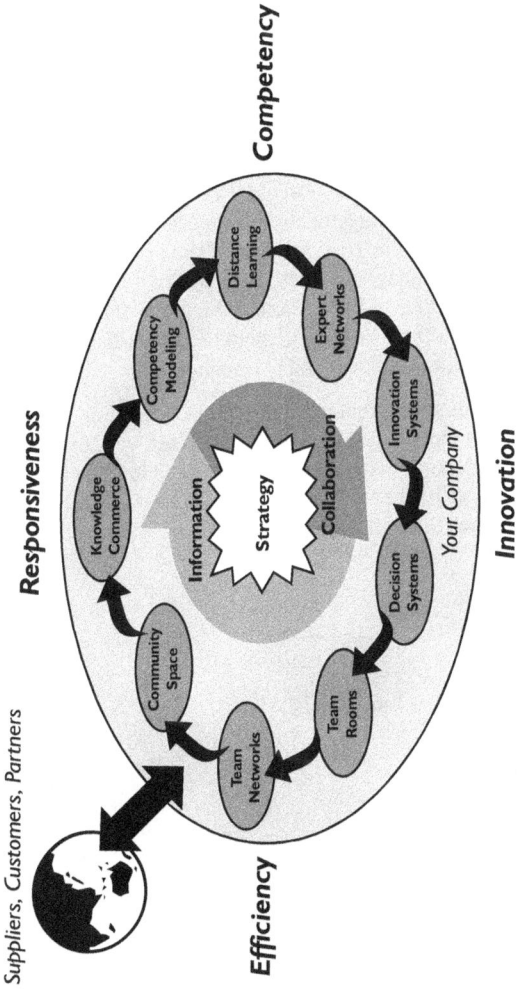

Competency

Responsiveness

Innovation

Efficiency

Suppliers, Customers, Partners

Distance Learning

Competency Modeling

Expert Networks

Knowledge Commerce

Innovation Systems

Information

Strategy

Collaboration

Community Space

Decision Systems

Your Company

Team Networks

Team Rooms

The large oval represents the company. The planet linked to the oval by a two-headed arrow represents customers, partners, suppliers, and others who are outside the company's boundaries, but linked to its success. Strategy, surrounded by Information and Collaboration, is at the center of this landscape. All knowledge management activities have to be tethered to the gravitational pull of the core corporate strategies. You don't want any runaway knowledge management projects drawing off resources and attention from the true business of the organization. And all knowledge management activities are built on a platform of information plus collaboration. Even those that are largely focused on information management require collaboration to be assembled, introduced, and maintained.

Orbiting around this center are several constellations of possible knowledge management initiatives. Each one relates to one of the four strategic knowledge management areas in the RICE model. We will describe them in a particular sequence, but they actually can be orchestrated in any order that fits the strategic imperatives. And they may not all fit into your unique corporate environment.

C = Competency

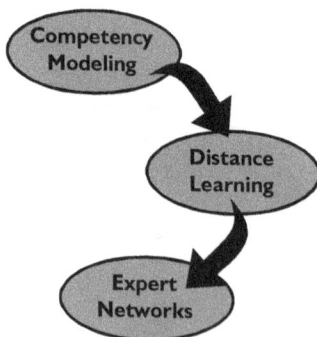

Competency modeling, distance learning, and expert networks focus on recognizing, developing, and improving the skill base of the workforce—spreading the know-how.

Competency Modeling. Once you have a clear vision of the strategic direction of the corporation and know what your core business is, you need to staff it with people who have the right skill sets. You will need systems and technology to accomplish three goals:

- Assessing the skill base of your current employees

- Providing the learning environments employees need to upgrade their skills

- Instituting systems for continually reassessing and advancing that skill base

A key first step is to know the current competency profile of the organization. In order to determine hiring needs, training needs, staffing directions, and career development, you need to know who knows what. And to prepare the organization for future growth in the knowledge arena and cultivate the right future capabilities, you need to know its current capabilities. A competency modeling initiative can have real strategic value, with visible and useful results. The company finds out where its intellectual capital strengths and deficits lie, and employees know which of their strengths fit the company's needs and which need developing.

Our hypothetical Vice President of Human Resources has primary responsibility for finding strong job candidates, hiring them, and training them. This is one of her top strategic imperatives. The company's leaders tacitly expect that employees' skills and competencies will keep pace as their jobs evolve. But they have not established objectives, formal processes, or ways to measure progress. The company has no systematic process in place for continuous assessment of employee competencies. Keeping employee skills at levels commensurate with changing job needs is more of a tacit expectation rather than a measured objective. Employees are told that they have five days of training available to them each year; but no one monitors whether the training days are used to train for tomorrow's job requirements—or even if they are used at all. And there is certainly no system in place for recognizing employees with valuable aptitudes and proactively providing them with the right education. Our VP is beginning to see a possible match between a competency modeling initiative and some of her objectives.

Distance Learning. Once you've made this competency assessment, you will need to find ways to upgrade and continually elevate the skill base of the organization. Particularly if you're a global, distributed company, you will need to find ways to provide this ongoing learning without continually having to remove people from their day-to-day work to bring them face-to-face for classroom teaching. Distance learning environments may become part of your strategy. Distance learning can be in the form of computer-based training in which an individual learns from a CD-ROM or a self-paced Web-based module at a desktop. Or, distance learning can be interactive and group-based using technology to create a virtual classroom with students in multiple locations and an instructor who can share a white board, manipulate objects, take quizzes, and post and respond to discussion points.

In large professional services firms, where at any given moment 50 percent of the workforce is either leaving or just coming on board, the need to retain knowledge and train new people rapidly requires some creative learning options. One option is an on-line education system that can provide employees with learning on their desktop computers, while they stay on the job. For example, if you're a consultant, you've just joined a new firm, and you are about to begin your first engagement, you can review a virtual, interactive module on contracting as you're about to set off for a meeting with your new customer.

Expert Networks. Once you have systems in place for assessing and upgrading the skill base of your workforce, you will have taken some large steps toward increasing the overall know-how of your people. Next, you will need a system for tracking and locating these highly skilled people—so you know where they are, what they're doing and learning, and how to find them. You have created a strong expertise base; now you need a way to tap into it, as needed.

As we discussed earlier, the knowledge needed to address changing customer and market shifts may not be located in any one document or report. That knowledge may be in tacit form, in the minds of several experts. Organizations need some form of expert networking system to track down the right people who have the right knowledge to contribute to a project team, make a high-level decision, or respond to a customer crisis.

A very simple version of an expert network or employee profiling system is the company white pages—a simple, searchable directory of names, locations, and reporting structures, preferably on-line. IBM's Blue Pages is such a system. These systems provide basic information, but are not very useful for helping a manager identify the right person to work on a particular, complex problem. Some systems include on-line resumes, a list of copyrights and patents won, and a list of most recent projects worked on. This is more useful, as long as it is on-line and searchable, but it is still static. The onus is on the employee to update the information, and that rarely happens.

Expert network systems are being developed that are capable of automatically culling relevant profiling data from existing sources and automatically keeping the employee profile current. With the employee's knowledge and approval, these systems can pull

79

relevant information from places such as other company databases, internal knowledge community websites, and the training and education system. These kinds of expert network systems enable managers to match employees with detailed work requirements—for example, someone with experience in both Web interface design and marketing in the Asia-Pacific region

So far, our Vice President of Human Resources is very interested in these three types of initiatives—Competency Modeling, Distance Learning, and Expert Network. She sees that these areas fall within her strategic objectives. They could add significant value to HR's contribution to keeping the company's overall know-how at high levels. She is eager to get started, but we would recommend that she subject her first impressions to a more rigorous due diligence.

I = Innovation

Innovation initiatives focus on the systems and technology that are concerned with developing new processes and products.

Innovation Systems. Once you have a skilled workforce continually upgrading its know-how, and you have a way of finding out who knows what and where these individuals are, you need to have this workforce doing work that increases the overall core competency of the organization. They need to be doing the work that keeps your company "best in the world" in its market. They need to be able to innovate to develop new products and new processes.

Innovation is actually a complex series of processes and will require several layers of support. On the cultural side of the spectrum, the corporate environment needs to be one in which new ideas are nourished, mistakes are not punished, and cross-pollination is encouraged. The overall culture needs to be one of knowledge sharing, not knowledge hoarding.

IBM Fellows Program

To encourage innovation, IBM launched a program for engineers who have been with the firm for fifteen years and who have a track record of creativity and productivity. They are given executive salaries and five years to work on whatever they want, with adequate resources.

In an innovative culture, employees need an idea collection and review system into which they can pump their new ideas. Many times a day, workers uncover challenges and come up with good ideas for addressing them. Most of these ideas are lost because no system exists for collecting them. One of the simplest things a company can do is institute an idea-harvesting system. If this system is electronic, employees can submit ideas anytime, anywhere, and the ideas can be searched, sorted, and organized easily. The following are key elements of such a system:

- It is accessible and easy to use

- All ideas are welcome

- A review process is in place to advance promising ideas beyond the suggestion stage to implementation

An innovation system also needs review and implementation components. A system must be in place to review ideas submitted and to assess them based on their potential for high value and their fit with corporate strategy. Promising ideas then need to be adequately funded and supported so that some of them can result in new or improved products and processes.

> ### *American Airlines—IdeAAs in Action*
>
> *American Airlines implemented a suggestion system that saved $83 million in the program's first two and a half years. In 1987, for example, a flight attendant passed along the observation that most passengers in First Class weren't eating the olives in their garden salads. American Airlines saved $440,000 by eliminating one olive from each salad served in First Class.*

Decision Systems. One could say that the business of management is to make decisions and to see that those decisions are turned into actions. Managers make dozens of decisions every day. Some of these fall within the scope of the manager's knowledge domain and sphere of influence and can be acted on relatively quickly. Many involve multiple fields of knowledge and several constituencies. If the innovation system is successful in eliciting a fruitful crop of new possibilities, tough decisions will have to be made about which projects to fund and resource. High-level decisions concerning global strategy, product direction, and sales and marketing systems are often so complex that expertise from outside the company needs to be brought in. And the window for making effective decisions opens and closes on Internet time and grows shorter as competitive challenges accelerate.

Decision systems help managers make sense out of data and information. They can involve both technology and community. The technology can help to analyze the layers of compound information that go into making complex decisions. And the community of decision-makers can apply their tacit understanding and personal experience base to make sense out of ever-changing information. Effective systems can help managers see intersecting information sets and patterns, track trends, make comparisons and benchmark, and even create scenarios. They can also help to surface critical inconsistencies and valuable new questions. Decision systems can be combined with an expert network system so that the right set of expertise is brought to bear on a problem.

E = Efficiency

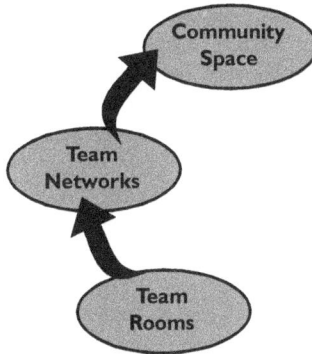

Efficiency initiatives focus on group collaboration to deliver value and to improve the existing processes of the organization. This is where people work, day to day, in teams and communities.

Team Rooms. Much of the day-to-day work of business happens in teams. Teams develop products, conduct research efforts, develop strategy, sell to customers, and engage in innumerable other activities. These days, teams are rarely together in one office where they can see each other any time. The globalization of companies and the ever-increasing pace of mergers and acquisitions and partnerships mean that team members are often spread across several regions and work in many functions and divisions.

The image of a team as a defined group of people hunkered down around a table committed to working on one project harks back to the height of the industrial era. In the Internet era, teams are dynamic, changing, mobile, and global. This represents a challenge. The players are often on the move, but the work still has to get done in a timely, efficient manner. Development teams at pharmaceutical companies are often composed of a core team of scientists dedicated to that product, along with a rotating membership of statisticians, legal consultants, and manufacturing representatives who spread themselves over several teams. Client engagement teams at professional services firms may have consultants from many regions—wherever the customer has offices—and will call in specialists as needed. Product development teams may outsource component parts of the overall work to other companies. Even teams that are located in one place may operate on shifts or have members who often travel. And, given the high turnover rate in many industries, you can count on team membership changing during the lifetime of any effort.

Technology can play a vital role in helping teams coordinate complex work across the boundaries of time and space. Teams often use a combination of tools to ensure the effective management of projects even though the team membership is distributed and changing.

In essence, just as co-located teams have had a "war room" which they can plaster with charts, schedules, and models; distributed teams need a virtual team room to help them coordinate the complex pieces of their overall project. We are using "room" as both a metaphor and an actuality. Teams need some space in which to work—be it a composite of several ingredients, or a full-scale virtual space. Some teams create this room using e-mail to communicate and maintain records. Others use a group calendar to share schedules and plan milestones and meetings. Many distributed teams are beginning to use virtual team spaces—electronic databases and websites—to share information, coordinate and track actions, and house their work products. These virtual teams call for new leadership styles and new team roles such as on-line team facilitator.

Teams can use any combination of the following tools:

- *Telephone conferencing*
- *Voicemail*
- *E-mail*
- *Virtual team rooms*
- *Videoconferencing*
- *Group calendaring and scheduling*
- *Workflow management and project management systems*
- *Chat*
- *Group meeting systems*

One of the advantages of using an electronic space that can retain a record of the team's work is that this record, in and of itself, often becomes an important knowledge artifact. The process a team used to reach key decisions, the record of those key decisions, the trail of actions assigned and actions completed, the results of experiments and conversations—all these elements represent the tacit knowledge of the team, now rendered explicit in an electronic container. Hallway conversations help only those who happen to participate. Virtual conversations and records can be there for future team members and future project teams to refer to. Wheels don't have to be reinvented if they have been archived and can be found and reused.

There is no one right team tool or tool set. The team and its managers will need to determine the media that best serve their needs. What is essential is that dynamic, global teams be provided with the electronic tools they need to get their jobs done. No tool, no matter how sophisticated, will turn a group into a high-performance team. A clear mission, along with clear objectives, goals, roles, and values, is the essence of team performance. Technology can help enable high performance, but it cannot inspire it.

Team Networks. Teams generally do not operate in isolation or as stand-alone units. A team is often part of a string of teams working in collaboration to deliver pieces of a larger whole. We call these strings of teams "team networks."

Team Networks need to:

- *Share best practices and models so that they leverage each other's learnings*
- *Get ideas from each other and learn about mistakes made*
- *Exchange status updates to ensure prompt handoffs*
- *Have a timely flow of information*
- *Plan meetings*
- *Reuse each others' materials so that they don't duplicate efforts*

An organization may have several teams working side by side on different components of one overall project. For example, at a pharmaceutical company, one team may be working on a solid form of a new drug while another is working on the liquid form. Or teams may work sequentially, with each team handing off its completed piece to the next team who adds subsequent components. One team may be assigned to the first version of a new product and a second team, perhaps with some of the same members, may come on board for the second revision.

The work of one team intertwines with the work of many others, at multiple points along the production continuum, working in related domains. A software product development effort involves a team network: teams who are coding, teams who are checking the code for errors (quality assurance), and teams who are creating the product documentation. Teams like these need to share information and knowledge. In fact, the efficiency of information exchange and collaboration among all the teams is essential to producing the desired results.

86

Breakdowns often occur at the intersections of these teams. Communication about expectations, deliverable schedules, and responsibilities sometimes gets lost in the space between teams. For example, if a software development team decides to shift directions in a feature set without the proper processes in place for informing the quality assurance team or the documentation team, those teams will lose valuable time working on outdated code. And more often than you might think, sale teams from the same company do not communicate with each other and end up pitching to the same customer and inadvertently underbidding and competing with each other.

These types of side-by-side teams need a system that supports interteam communication and collaboration. And managers who are responsible for the big picture need a way to manage information and activity flow across teams. Again, technology can play a pivotal role. Systems can be set up that automatically notify a team member, a manager, or the entire team when a critical decision has been made that has cross-team impact or when one team requires an action by another to reach a critical project deadline. Postings from one team's virtual work space that are red alerts to other teams in the network can automatically appear in those teams' virtual space or in their e-mail. Key learnings, or knowledge nuggets, created and posted in one team's work space can be flagged and harvested to a communal team space so that all interested parties can benefit. With team networks, as with teams, technology cannot substitute for well-thought-out process and cultural considerations. Teams need to be willing to collaborate and understand their shared objectives if technology is to add value.

Community Space. Communities have always existed as a means for people to make connections around common interests and leverage the strength of many—from medieval craft guilds to modern urban neighborhood watches. Communities are nothing new. What *is* new is that corporations are recognizing the tremendous advantage the community concept offers as a strategic advantage.

Communities in organizations become hubs of knowledge exchange. They are the meeting place, physical and virtual, for people with shared interests and practices to come together for their benefit, each other's benefit—and the company's benefit. In an unpredictable, fluid, global environment in which the strategic direction, the players, and the very boundaries of the organization can blur and shift without much warning, communities become home base and are often where people go to learn about the organization and to master the tools of their trade. A new regional sales manager in a consumer products company needs to know who's who, how things get done, and how other sales managers become successful. She is not likely to get the full information picture from her boss, her subordinates, or Human Resources. She needs to find and plug into the informal communities in her areas of practice that will help her come up to speed as quickly as possible and begin to form the essential ongoing connections she will need to stay successful. She needs communities.

A Community-Building Solution

A 40 person community of innovation in the rail car industry used Communispace, a web-based system of software and services, to come together virtually. In less than a week's time, they generated over 186 new ideas to create the rail car of the future.

Communities are the social infrastructure of ongoing knowledge creation and exchange. They focus on enhancing overall know-how and core competencies, not on building a specific product. Engineers at Royal Dutch/Shell meet to discuss innovations in deep-water drilling. Engineers at DaimlerChrysler transfer their lessons learned across the company. Scientists in specialty fields at IBM Research share findings and provide consultations across geographies. Xerox repair technicians share their war stories and lessons learned to create a dynamic learning system that far surpasses the static technician repair manual. These are all examples of corporate communities that serve social, learning, and strategic purposes.

Communities provide links among moving targets and pathways through shifting organizational sands. They last longer than teams, and often longer than some departments. While its membership may change, the community itself persists, and can be the continuous learning environment in the ever-changing corporate landscape.

Benefits of Communities

By creating informal opportunities for people to connect, communities serve to:

- *Bring forward tacit, previously unexpressed knowledge, expressing it and making it widely usable*
- *Create ongoing channels for learning across organizational boundaries such as divisions, functions (accounting, marketing, sales, purchasing), and regions*
- *Provide broader reaching networking opportunities—for senior and junior staff who may not otherwise have access to each other*
- *Offer opportunities for mentoring and ongoing learning*
- *Create proving grounds for testing, verifying, and spreading newly coined best practices*
- *Provide more opportunities for serendipity to occur—fortuitous, random encounters of ideas and people that can lead to unanticipated creativity and innovation*

And—very importantly—communities can span companies, vendors and suppliers, and the organization and its customers, creating new opportunities for mutual advantage.

Communities exist naturally in organizations. Managers need to determine which of these contribute to enhancing the corporate culture, organizational learning, and organizational core competence. For these valuable, self-seeding kinds of communities, corporate policy and managers need to offer sustenance in two forms:

- Providing resources—meeting rooms, databases, time and funding for conferences, online community facilitators, etc.

- Reducing interference—preventing people from trying to manage communities as if they were projects. A more organic approach is required in which the natural momentum of the community is the driver, not management by directive.

Managers may also be able to catalyze potential new communities into life. Starting new communities can be difficult. They often show initial promise, then quickly fizzle. Buckman Labs has been successful at creating communities that share innovative ways of solving customer problems. Some professional service firms have created communities in specialty practice areas to share best practices. The organization can emphasize the strategic value of this new community, find talented allies and proponents, and fund a kick-off meeting where people can meet face to face. Then it is up to the community members to find their own ongoing purpose and process.

Technology as an enabler of ongoing communication is very valuable in helping to maintain the cohesiveness of the community over time and space. Communities, like teams, need contact to rekindle the social links. Especially if the community is large and widely distributed geographically, face-to-face opportunities are rare and expensive. Technology can:

- Provide various settings for large and smaller group interests

- Enable large group discussions and one-to-one chat

- Offer on-line learning modules

- House a library of materials relevant to the community

- House an archive of community artifacts and products that may be of value to new members and to the larger organization.

A Community Space technology can help a diverse community stay focused and connected and can become a greenhouse of reusable knowledge assets.

R = Responsiveness

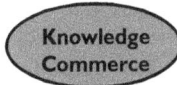

Knowledge Commerce

Responsiveness activities are concerned with taking in information from the marketplace and using that information to respond to customer interests.

Knowledge Commerce. Knowledge commerce is a vast realm, encompassing areas such as e-business, business-to-business, employee-to-business, and customer relationship management. Knowledge commerce refers to those initiatives that leverage Internet (and extranet) capabilities to sense and respond rapidly to customer and market shifts and take advantage of emergent business opportunities.

Scanning for Emerging Trends

Nokia, a Finnish telecommunications company, for many years had a program in place called Future Watch. Future Watch involved people from many different sectors of the organization, working globally in virtual spaces, focused on scanning the environment for emergent customer trends and technological advances that could keep Nokia product development ahead of the competitive curve.

91

Knowledge commerce activities can exist within the organization. More importantly, they link the organization to the outside world (in what is often called e-business)—to its customers, other businesses, vendors, suppliers, partners, and to potential new collaborators. In a recent survey, the Gartner Group predicted that Internet-based business-to-business activities—a $145 billion market in 1999—will reach $7.29 trillion worldwide by 2004. (The total amount of all business-to-business sales last year was $14 trillion.)[2]

Knowledge commerce activities are varied. Business-to-business commerce, such as supply chains, use the Internet to link multiple players in series of complex interactions. Manufacturers can interact directly with consumers, distributors with suppliers, and consumers with each other. Customer relationship management systems can keep customer knowledge and industry research fresh and available to all who need it.

The magazine *Fast Company* has created a community of its readers who interact with each other and with staff on its website. This not only draws readers closer to the magazine, but can also serve as an early detection system alerting editors to the latest reader interests and reactions. Hyundai uses a B2B system to stay closer to its dealers and enable them to see regular updates in its catalogue and learn about special dealer-only inventory and promotion offers. Honeywell is implementing a B2B Internet ordering system for the auto dealers, parts distributors, lube centers, and retail chains that stock its consumer products. On the buyer side, General Motors, Ford, and DaimlerChrysler are setting up an e-marketplace for their suppliers. Currently, these three companies spend $240 billion a year on the parts and materials they buy from suppliers.[3]

Knowledge commerce can also include the development of new knowledge internally which then becomes available to the marketplace. The knowledge that companies produce as part of their day-to-day operations can develop into new, sellable products or services. The Balanced Scorecard, for example, was developed for business clients by Robert S. Kaplan, a Harvard Business School professor and David H. Norton, a management consultant. They have evolved the approach into a consulting product which they license to certain consulting firms. Lotus Institute, an R&D facility within Lotus/IBM, developed a tool (TeamRoom) and a process for helping to better orchestrate the work of internal teams and task forces. The design principles and the implementation methodology that were refined internally evolved into new product offerings for customers: a new template included with the core product offering and a stand-alone hostable team tool, Quickplace.

By now, you are probably beginning to consider some of these possibilities for your own organization. For our new VP of Human Resources, it is becoming clear that competency modeling, distance learning, and an expert network could be valuable initiatives. She is also wondering if spearheading a company-wide program to accelerate virtual teaming might integrate Human Resources even more fully into the day-to-day processes of the business.

Take a Moment

Take a moment to note which of these areas are beginning to seem more likely candidates for your own organization's knowledge management focus.

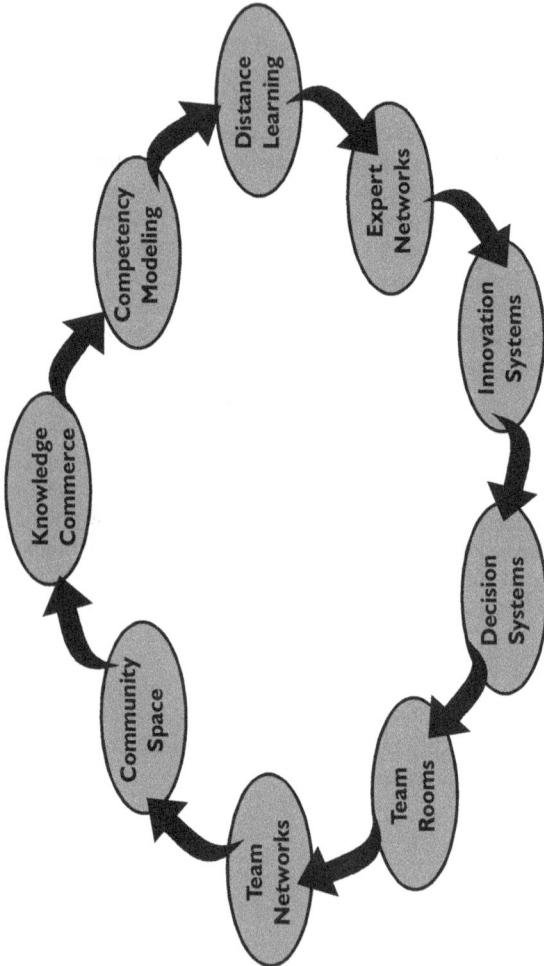

Consider the following list of questions as you begin to construct your own knowledge management strategy:

1. **Strategy**
   - What is your current position in the marketplace? Are you exploiting existing opportunities and/or exploring new innovative possibilities?
   - What is your unique core competence? What do you need to do to solidify and extend it?
   - Is there a mandate to see knowledge as a key corporate asset and to manage it energetically?
   - Do the organization and senior management demonstrate a commitment to ongoing organizational learning?
   - Where are your first-strike knowledge management initiatives most likely to produce valuable and visible results? Internally? With customers?
   - Where do you need to begin to plant the seeds for longer-term, more extensive knowledge management projects?

2. **Knowledge**
   - What percentage of your knowledge assets is already expressed? And accessible?
   - Are there processes in place for capturing expressible knowledge?
   - Are there forums in place (face-to-face and virtual) for sustaining community interaction?
   - Do you have sufficient knowledge assets in the three key areas of *Know-What, Know-Who,* and *Know-How*? Where are the deficits?

3. **Culture**

- Does your culture lean more toward knowledge sharing or knowledge hoarding?

- Are mistake making and risk taking suspicious activities or seen as learning opportunities?

- Are there resources in place and roles defined for managing your knowledge assets?

- Are people rewarded for contributing to the knowledge capital of your organization?

- Are there measures in place for assessing the impact of knowledge contributions and initiatives?

4. **Technology**

- Do you have the needed infrastructure capability to support knowledge management systems?

- Do you have tools and training available to make packaged knowledge easily accessible?

- Are there tools and training available to support virtual team work and community collaboration?

Recap

This chapter focused on how to launch a knowledge management initiative. It builds on the RICE model—Responsiveness, Innovation, Competency, and Efficiency. We have explored how a manager charged with launching knowledge management can focus on nine specific action areas linked to each part of the RICE model. These action areas provide targeted ways to assess and build competency, use knowledge to make processes more efficient, increase responsiveness, and nurture innovation.

Endnotes

[1] James Brian Quinn, "Strategic Outsourcing: Leveraging Knowledge Capabilities," *Sloan Management Review,* Summer 1999, 9–21.

[2] Michelle Delio, "Bridging B2B with B2E," *Knowledge Management*, May 2000, 18; Louis Uchitelle, "Business to Business; It's Just the Beginning," *New York Times*, June 7, 2000.

[3] "Business to Business: It's Just the Beginning," *New York Times*, June 7, 2000.

Chapter 6
Implementing Knowledge
Management

Now that we have explored the knowledge landscape and looked at knowledge management initiatives in the areas of *responsiveness, innovation, competency,* and *efficiency,* you are probably honing in on how to institute knowledge management practices in your organization. In this chapter, we will look at how to do that by walking you through best-practice processes and then exploring a knowledge management implementation scenario at a hypothetical company.

Best Practice Processes

1. *Define the Business Need.* The practices that you are considering should address a real business need—a "need to have," not a "nice to have." Your responses to the questions at the end of Chapter 5 can help you assess priorities and think about the feasibility of initiating a knowledge management project within your company's environment—given its strengths, weaknesses, and available financial and human resources. For example, if your strategy demands that a significant percentage of revenue come from products under two years old, then you need to invest not only in R&D but in a coherent knowledge management system that accelerates innovation.

   Don't be seduced by amazing technology. Allow your visionary faculties to be tickled by remarkable technology;

but ground your excitement in the business actualities of your organization—your current needs and needs that lie around the curve.

Many companies and CIOs have come to regret purchasing fancy IT systems that have theoretical promise but don't deliver in their particular environment. Technology can enable you to set up virtual meetings with chat, video contact, shared white boards, and shared documents which multiple parties can see and edit. People can participate from their desktops anywhere in the world. However, if, in your culture, people put a high value on face-to-face interaction or do not share works in progress, only finished products, then they may not be ready for virtual collaboration technology. Technology can help you create wild multimedia presentations with spinning, flashing objects and high-quality sound and music with dramatic sound bites thrown in. But if these capabilities do not suit your marketing strategy or your corporate image, then they are irrelevant.

2. *Ensure Sufficient Support.* For an initiative to get off the ground and really fly, it needs support from four sources:

   - executive sponsors
   - an operations leader
   - the employees
   - resources

The executive sponsor blesses the project, funds it, and keeps it visible at high levels. The operations leader defines its scope, fires up the troops, oversees project management, and runs interference. These people need to be believers and communicate the real business value of the initiative up and down the corporate ladder. As for employees—the people who will be affected by the initiative—involving them early is essential for assessing their real, urgent work needs and setting their expectations about impending changes. Early and ongoing inclusion of employees in defining their own work processes can go a long way toward preventing later mutiny.

The resources you need are adequate funding and sufficient time from those who will be involved in the project. We have seen too many knowledge management initiatives get launched and then dwindle because no one is designated to remain at the helm and no one is assigned to continue to work at the day-to-day level. An initiative doesn't necessarily require people's full-time attention. But it does require some percentage of people's work time. You can't expect an enthusiastic employee to do a "real" full-time job and keep up a knowledge management role on top of that. Knowledge management roles have to be integrated into "real" work.

In addition, the funding has to support any additional technical infrastructure needed to host the initiative, as well as new technology, applications, or consulting. Training will likely be needed and must also be factored into the funding equation.

3. *Begin with Piloting—Learn as You Go.* A knowledge management initiative represents a tremendous learning opportunity—from a technical, a process, and a cultural perspective. Typically, you should begin with a pilot project, and call it that. Calling it "pilot" gives you attention and permission to learn—two useful ingredients. It is important to design the pilot project with a "learn as you go" protocol or intentional experimentation in mind.

Experimentation does not mean shooting knowledge darts blindly at a blank screen and hoping that they spell out some business success formula. Experimentation means that you begin, as you would any serious project, with careful scoping, thoughtful process design, and inclusion of all the key players. Experimentation means keeping a constant observing eye across all aspects of the project, noting and documenting what's working and what's not. And what's not working needs to be adjusted during the course of the project, not just at the end. We call this an iterative learning process—try, learn, adjust, try—and it is essential for knowledge management projects.

For the first few pilots, target the low hanging fruit.

- Focus on an urgent, current business need that is neither too complex nor too multilayered to be solved
- Find solutions to real, noticeable problems
- Pick efforts that have a high chance of success for the company and the individuals involved
- Seek outcomes with measurable impact and clear results

A successful knowledge management project that truly helps people work smarter provides momentum for future initiatives. The best PR comes from employees and customers who say, "This made a real difference in helping me get what I need."

4. *Building on the Initial Pilots.* The piloting and iterative learning process are essential. As you consider pilot opportunities, you will also need to think about the "big picture," and consider the overall knowledge management landscape. You will need to engage other champions, visionaries, and leaders in mapping out the larger strategy. Think of the pilots as catalysts for a more comprehensive, organization-wide strategy. And each part of the wider strategy should likewise begin with a pilot learning phase. The learning needs to continue and be incorporated into the ongoing planning and deployment—as we illustrate in a sidebar on an actual knowledge management pilot project and an indepth scenario about knowledge management at a hypothetical pharmaceutical products company.

102

Learning from the Pilot: One Story

Lotus Institute partnered in a knowledge management pilot project with the tax practice of a large consulting firm. New ideas make money in the tax field. Ideas in the international tax field have short lifespans because tax laws are always changing. The concept is to come up with new ideas for investing or saving money before tax and revenue services can close the loophole you're using. A good, unique, timely idea can represent a huge financial advantage. And several resulted from this project.

The knowledge management initiative was focused on innovation and idea generation and used a new Notes-based technology to enable a group of global specialists, each in a different geographic region, to share virtually and build on each other's ideas.

Learnings from the pilot were as valuable as its success:

- *While this company had been using Notes for many years, it was a mistake to assume that each participant was comfortable enough with the technology to use it in this new way. Some participants dropped out for that reason.*

- *The infrastructure did not support immediate transmission of postings around the world. An idea posted in New York could take a few days to reach the Notes-based application on the company's Singapore server. This delay made it hard for everyone to stay in the loop. This was an important discovery with implications beyond the scope of the pilot.*

- *More junior staff welcomed the opportunity to virtually interact with senior staff with whom they would otherwise rarely have a chance to meet. Senior staff also preferred to interact with other senior staff members and saw value in having access to their equal expert peers around the world.*

(continued)

Learning from the Pilot: One Story (concluded)

- *Time and attention are the most precious commodity of all. While the participants saw the value of participating during the pilot period, their "day jobs" eventually won out over this new initiative. Because the initiative never became part of their regular work, the gravitational pull of day-to-day demands left them with too little time and attention to continue after the pilot stage. So, while the operation was a success (and money was made), the patient died (in that participants were pulled away by other projects and did not push to sustain the approach past the pilot stage).*

During the course of the pilot, we observed, modified the application, tried to address infrastructure hurdles, and kept in contact with all participants to hear their ideas about how to improve the project in process. The learnings from this pilot informed future revisions of the application and the methodology for deployment, including the development of on-line training in creative thinking and cultural assessment and change management components.

A Scenario for Launching Knowledge Management

Our hypothetical company, Bio-Brand, is a mid-sized pharmaceutical products company with a reputation for being highly innovative. It has had major success with a small portfolio of drugs and has been riding that success for many years. However, the end of its patent protection period is approaching.

Bio-Brand's continued success in this business environment depends on its ability to leverage its scientific and research capability to create new products and receive patents on new formulas—and reduce the amount of time it takes to do so. While the long-term profit margins on a successful, patented drug are high, the time to patent for Bio-Brand products has been nine to twelve years. The company needs to reduce this barrier to entry to seven to eight years.

Another key to success is getting expertise either from new hires or by acquiring small start-up companies who have specialty products or components and the experts who can develop them further. The people who are hired into Bio-Brand are highly educated M.D.s and Ph.D.s, and other professionals, with established networks among scientists and researchers around the world. The market for these people is very competitive and a high-quality R&D environment is crucial to attracting and retaining them. Bio-Brand finds recruiting and retaining high-level talent to be a challenge. In addition, it takes six to nine months to fully orient and train a new hire. And staff tenure ranges from a high of twelve years to an increasing low of two years. Bio-Brand needs to better understand its increasing attrition rate and do more to retain staff.

As Bio-Brand grows by entering new markets and through hiring and acquisition, it is becoming increasingly global. Clinical teams now have members from several geographies and from several different, now merged, companies. The firm's customer base is also increasingly global and its sales strategy is no longer purely regional. Bio-Brand now sells products to a managed care consortium with facilities throughout the United States and Canada. A team composed of sales reps from many different areas will work together to sell to their global customers. These teams need to learn how to work collaboratively while remaining geographically separated. And, as new clinical and sales teams form, they need to leverage existing protocols and methodologies and materials, rather than reinventing wheels.

Bio-Brand's products currently compete on uniqueness and quality, but a number of firms are revving up to copy Bio-Brand's products once their patents lapse. Because of this competition, in addition to keeping new drugs in its development pipeline, Bio-Brand wants to develop value-added service offerings that can be packaged with its products. For example, Bio-Brand is sending its senior researchers into the field as on-site advisors to doctors as they test new drugs and medical products in trials. In this way, doctors, who are the firm's key customers, get immediate access to expertise and Bio-Brand researchers get immediate feedback on their products. This serves to increase customer loyalty and keep senior scientists fresh and full of new real world ideas that might turn into new product ideas. However, this strategy, while having demonstrated value, relies on face-to-face contact and takes up the valuable research time of Bio Brands senior staff. Additional, more innovative means of reaching the customer need to be developed.

The executive leadership group has been meeting to review these challenges. They see them as challenges to the ways Bio-Brand addresses its knowledge management capabilities: their "Know-What," "Know-Who," and "Know-How." The leadership group has identified the following six key areas for knowledge management initiatives:

- Reducing time to patent through better management of information

- Attracting and retaining high-caliber scientific and sales talent

- Reducing new employee time to productivity

- Enabling distributed teams to work collaboratively on complex projects

- Enabling broad communities of knowledge workers, within and outside the company, to interact

- Creating innovative value-added service components as part of the customer relationship management process

106

A Structured Strategy. Using the RICE model, the leadership team organizes the issues, laying the groundwork for a focused, manageable, accountable process:

Responsiveness

- Creating innovative value-added service components as part of their customer relationship management process

Innovation

- Reducing time to patent through better management of information

Competency

- Attracting and retaining high-caliber scientific and sales talent
- Reducing new employee time to productivity

Efficiency

- Enabling distributed teams to work collaboratively on complex projects
- Enabling broad communities of knowledge workers, within and outside the company, to interact

Each area is to be actively managed by one "champion" from the leadership group. The champion will work with the lead operations manager to address the strategy, knowledge, culture, and technology questions listed in Chapter 5. This gives the leadership group a stable foundation for proceeding and prevents them from jumping prematurely to a pure technology response before the environment is ready to effectively use it. The answers to these questions will help them determine what steps may need to be undertaken—before or during a knowledge management pilot—to ready the organization to use knowledge management as part of its way of doing business.

Each area begins with a pilot program that will provide visible and valuable results and will be overseen by the champion and staffed by the operations manager and a dedicated team. They will be responsible for shaping and rolling out a knowledge management pilot. They can use the knowledge management landscape (also described in Chapter 5) to help them think about possible initiatives. Each initiative on the landscape will need to be fully scoped out from a business value, a cultural, a process, and a technology perspective.

For example, if the team is working on *enabling broad communities of knowledge workers, within and outside the company, to interact*, they begin by doing an assessment that includes issues such as these:

1. Does our company believe in the business value of communities, and is our company a nourishing place for communities to grow?

2. What communities would ideally serve the best strategic interests of the company? Do they already exist?

3. What communities currently exist naturally inside of the company?

4. What communities currently exist that span the boundaries of the company?

5. Are existing communities of strategic value? If so, do they have the resources they need to be effective; and are there processes in place to funnel some of their knowledge products back to the company?

6. If appropriate communities don't exist, could the company foster their emergence?

The team plans to consider and manage issues such as cultural compatibility between the company and the community; respect for the integrity of the community; and agreements with the community to harvest and use some of its tacit and explicit knowledge products. Is there sufficient motivation for people to participate? Do specific community roles need to be supported, such as facilitator, knowledge harvester, and administrator?

The team will also consider what form of technology would best support the many needs of the community from functional and infrastructure perspectives. Functional considerations include:

- Storing knowledge
- Engaging in multiple dialogue types
- Profiling members
- Filtering information
- General administration
- Engaging in knowledge work processes (such as decision making, brainstorming, and identifying action steps)

Infrastructure considerations include the platform, firewall issues, and scalability.

The project team, after reviewing its assessment of these and other issues, decides on the processes and technology needed for piloting a community space knowledge management initiative. They will need to set up success criteria for the pilot and monitor the initiative throughout its duration. They will need to use the iterative learning process described earlier in this chapter (try, learn, adjust, try) and be sure to stay in contact with users and make modifications as needed along the way. They will also need to communicate their learnings, successes, and obstacles to their champion, who can begin to spread news of the value of the initiative to other arenas.

Bio-Brand's Experience with Piloting a Community Space

Bio-Brand is fortunate in that there are already a number of active, successful, and strategic communities. Most of them are communities of researchers who exchange findings and use each other as ad hoc advisors. Many of the queries begin with "Have you ever seen this before... or had this result?" Or, "Do you know where I can find this piece of equipment?" Individual managers see the value in these exchanges and support employees spending time in communities. These communities tend to be small, with membership spreading by word or mouth, and they use list servs as their communications vehicle. Community members speak highly of their activity in their communities and consider it important to their ongoing development. New employees who stumble into a community are excited to have the opportunity to learn so much so quickly and to interact with the experts.

For Bio-Brand, the challenge is to take these communities out of the closet and expand their potential without damaging their momentum. Working with community members, the team decides that providing communities with a more robust, collaborative form of technology that could meet more of their needs (for sharing documents, collaborating on papers and projects, etc.) would be of significant value. Bio-Brand also offers to host all these communities and put a directory of communities on its company intranet so more people could learn of their existence and join. The project team works with each community to design processes for ensuring that new members have the appropriate skills and job requirements to participate and that they are trained to use the community space technology. Bio Brand also offers a cadre of trained virtual facilitators to each community who can help facilitate conversations and may also serve as links to others.

They can flag information as having knowledge value to the company or to other communities and bring in useful information from other communities.

The success of communities in the research area sparks interest in other parts of the company. Sales and marketing teams, already comfortable working as distributed teams in virtual spaces, want to form communities of interest to share leads and best practices more broadly. Bio-Brand is able to leverage its learnings from its early pilot experiences and use them to bootstrap the formation of new communities.

Bio-Brand is also in the process of setting up communities with customers, as one part of its initiative to offer customers value-added services. This will be a space in which customers can get immediate responses to their questions and concerns and know that they are being heard. Bio-Brand will benefit from early warnings about what really matters to its customers.

So far, the biggest hurdle Bio-Brand has faced in creating communities is in linking up with researchers in other companies. The legal issues concerning protected information and technical firewall issues have made this a difficult challenge, and, for the time being, the company is focusing on other knowledge management areas where more immediate results can be won.

Recap

Stephen Covey, author of *The 7 Habits of Highly Effective People,* advises beginning with the end in mind. With knowledge management, begin with strategy in mind. Start by assessing the business value of the potential initiative. Thinking about your core competencies helps map how knowledge management can add value to your business. As we discussed in Chapter 5, core competencies fall into four main target areas:

- **R**esponsiveness to the market
- **I**nnovation of new products and services
- **C**ompetency of your skill base
- **E**fficiency of work processes

One or more of these dimensions will be likely candidate areas for your knowledge management initiatives. Within each dimension, decide which practical application of knowledge management will create visible and valuable results. We offered you many options in Chapter 5.

Pick a real business need that will, when addressed, get people's notice. It needs to be one that can be addressed and measured in a visible way and within a realistic time frame. This is also the time to consider the cultural and process issues you will face in your organization. Line up leaders and resources. Then consider technology. Addressing technology at this point ensures that it will serve your project, not drive it.

Once you've chosen your target area (e.g., Efficiency) and application focus (e.g., Community Space), begin with a pilot that will permit you to both accomplish some real objective and learn as you proceed.

At the same time, you will need to consider the "big picture" and the other critical areas for embedding knowledge management into your business. A successful initial pilot can serve as fuel for expanding your knowledge management efforts and for engaging the support of other key players. Each additional knowledge management effort should begin with a pilot phase that permits you to learn as you go and incorporate those learnings into your ongoing and future efforts.

The following outline can serve as a road map:

Stages of Knowledge Management Strategy

Assessment
- *Core competencies—strengths, deficits, and challenges*
- *Real business needs—external and internal*
- *Culture—strengths and challenges*
- *High value/high visibility opportunities for knowledge management initiatives*
- *Resources—leadership and funding*
- *Infrastructure and technology*

Planning
- *Pilot opportunities*
- *Big picture strategy*
- *Staging of both*
- *Learning strategy*
- *Measures of success*
- *Technical readiness*

Deployment
- *Pilot(s)*
- *Communication about pilots and larger strategy*

Evaluation
- *Pilots—during and after*
- *Organizational readiness to proceed*
- *Technical readiness to proceed*
- *Next pilot opportunities*

Recommended Reading

Davenport, Thomas H., and Laurence Prusak. *Working Knowledge—How Organizations Manage What they Know.* Boston: Harvard Business School Press, 1998.

Leonard, Dorothy. *Wellsprings of Knowledge—Building and Sustaining the Sources of Innovation.* Boston: Harvard Business School Press, 1995.

Nonaka, Ikujiro, and Hirotaka Takeuchi. *The Knowledge Creating Company.* New York: Oxford University Press, 1995.

Senge, Peter M. *The Fifth Discipline: The Art and Practice of the Learning Organization.* New York: Doubleday, 1994.

Utterback, James M. *Mastering the Dynamics of Innovation— How Companies Can Seize Opportunities in the Face of Technological Change.* Boston: Harvard Business School Press, 1994.

Weick, Karl E. *Sensemaking in Organizations.* Thousand Oaks, California: Sage Publications, 1995.

About the Authors

Kathleen Foley Curley is currently Senior Vice President and Chief Community Builder at Communispace Corporation. Before joining Communispace, she was Chief Knowledge Management strategist for the IBM Software Group where she was responsible for articulating and integrating the knowledge management and e-business strategies for this $14 billion division. Before joining the IBM Software Group, Curley was Executive Director of the Lotus Institute. Her work focused on knowledge management and the integration of people, processes, and technologies to foster the creation and sharing of knowledge to support a learning organization. Specific Lotus products that were launched from Lotus Institute include TeamRoom, Lotus LearningSpace, and Raven, Lotus's knowledge management platform currently under development.

Curley received her MBA and DBA degrees from Harvard Business School and an undergraduate degree in Economics from Smith College. She has published in academic and practitioner journals including the *Sloan Management Review*, *MIS Quarterly, Datamation,* and *The Journal of Global Information Systems*. Before joining the Lotus Institute, Curley was a tenured professor in the MIS department at Northeastern University's College of Business Administration, a Visiting Scholar at MIT's Center for Information Systems Research, and a curriculum advisor to The Arthur D. Little School of Management. She has consulted in the areas of business and technology strategy and in the strategic application of expert systems for such clients as American Express, Bristol Myers Squibb, Stone and Webster, and British Airways.

Barbara Kivowitz is president of the BEK Group, a consulting consortium based in Brookline, Massachusetts, that provides change management and collaborative technology consulting. She helps companies create knowledge management and organizational learning solutions that emphasize collaborative practices which are often enabled by technology. She specializes in strategies for creating sustainable results in the areas of organizational learning, virtual collaboration (particularly distributed team and community performance), global leadership excellence, and creativity and innovation practices. She is also Vice President of Learning Strategies at a startup e-learning company.

Prior to founding the BEK group, Kivowitz was the Chief Organizational Systems Architect for Lotus Institute, part of Lotus/IBM. Lotus Institute was an advanced R&D group dedicated to designing solutions in the areas of knowledge management, virtual collaboration, and distance learning. She was responsible for designing the methodological components of many of Lotus Institute's solutions in addition to contributing to technology design. She was also the principal manager of their creativity and innovation solution area. She has written articles and white papers on virtual teaming, technology-enabled innovation, and knowledge management.

Her background is in the fields of psychology and social systems theory, and she holds graduate degrees from Harvard University and Simmons College. She can be reached at bkivowitz@post.harvard.edu.

Index